Necessary

Journeys

Necessary Journeys

Letting Ourselves Learn From Life

Nancy L. Snyderman, M.D.,
and Peg Streep

HYPERION
New York

Wes, Lisa + Suzann Its all about the journey.

[signature]

Book design by Richard Oriolo

FIRST EDITION

10   9   8   7   6   5   4   3   2   1

Contents

To the circle of women who have stood by me,

especially when I lost my way,

and to Kate, Rachel, Charlie, and Doug,

my everyday reminders of how

deliciously lucky I am.

No matter how much women prefer to lean, to be protected and supported, nor how much men prefer to have them do so, they must make the voyage of life alone, and for safety in an emergency they must know something of the laws of navigation.

—ELIZABETH CADY STANTON, 1892

A Necessary Journey

❧

I NEVER EXPECTED life to be so messy.

If a palm reader had studied my hand while I was growing up and told me that, along with becoming a doctor and a television correspondent, I'd be married three times, go broke once, start my life over alone with two children in a brand-new city at the age of thirty-six, and, finally, end up personally happy in my forties as a wife and mother of three, I would have yanked my hand back and rolled my eyes. And asked for a refund.

But she would have been right, after all.

Of course, I didn't know any palm readers in Fort Wayne, Indiana, where I grew up, amid miles of rolling hills and fertile farmland, dotted every now and then with a white farmhouse and a red barn. The housing developments and strip malls that have since gobbled up the farms weren't a part of life in America's heartland then, and every street and store had its own personality. Now, when I go back and the commuter plane circles the airport, I find myself pressing my face against the window, searching for the landmarks that tell me I'm home. Each time, I'm disappointed to see that more of them are gone. The child in me wants "home" to be the way it always was.

Fort Wayne wasn't a place I ever remember planning on leaving, not consciously at least. Actually, I'm not really sure I "planned" anything all that far into the future. I simply assumed that my life would be just like my parents' life and the progression of my childhood: neat and orderly. Life in Fort Wayne was solid, and it still is. My best friends from my childhood and my adolescence still live there, as do my parents. All these years later, I'm still close to Mike, my best friend in high school, and, over the course of visits, his kids and mine have become friends. I go back every year for the Fourth of July and the parade is just as I remember it.

I lived in the same house from the time I was one

until I turned seventeen, in a neighborhood where no one had fences and kids ran from yard to yard, and everyone's mom knew you and your mom. I guess I was relatively privileged—my dad was a doctor and belonged to the local country club—but my family lived an unpretentious life, and I grew up feeling very much a part of the fabric of life in a small Midwestern city.

I live in San Francisco now, a beautiful and romantic city perched on a bay that looks just like the postcards hundreds of thousands of tourists send home every year. It is the city I moved to to rebuild my life and reinvent myself just over ten years ago, as a single mother of two. Much more than miles separates my children's hometown from the one I grew up in. The woman who is a mother and wife, doctor and television correspondent isn't the same person as the girl who lived and dreamed about her future in Fort Wayne. But as much as the experiences of the roads I've traveled since leaving home have shaped me, Fort Wayne and what growing up there taught me are also a part of the fabric of my soul. Going back to Fort Wayne has always grounded me, and I've made it a point to make sure my children, who live a privileged life in a cosmopolitan city, understand my Indiana roots.

Even though much has changed in Fort Wayne since my girlhood, and my parents moved to a fancier, more modern house twenty years ago, the one-story ranch house I grew up in still stands among the same houses, still painted the same colors, in my old neighborhood. The fir tree I climbed both as a tomboy and, later, as a teenager desperate for space and a view of the world, still towers over the hill. Even so, I know exactly how long I've been gone and how many miles away I've traveled when I look at the tree my parents planted in the front yard when I was six. The once sunny lawn is now cast into shade by its leaves and branches, and my mother's carefully tended strawberry patch has long since been taken over by lawn.

A few years ago, I drove by the house, as I always do when I'm in Fort Wayne, but this time it had a "For Sale" sign out in front. For years, I fantasized about walking through the house again, just to relive some of my childhood memories and maybe even get in touch with my girlhood self who'd been so happy there. I called the real estate agent and, of course, he was happy to let me see it. I asked my mom if she wanted to come, but she thought it'd be too sad, something that puzzled me at the time but that doesn't any longer. Instead, I took my oldest daughter, Kate, eager to show her where my stories took place. I imagined myself giving her the tour: Here's the trellis to the roof my sister and I climbed when we hid from our brothers; this is the living room where your grandmother stopped the fight between your uncles when they were boys and broke her finger in the process; this was my room and it was painted white.

The rooms were smaller and the ceilings lower than I remembered, and the woods that separated the back yard from the highway were shorter and thinner than the childhood forest stored in my memory. But the warmth and love of the family I grew up in seemed, to me at least, still to be a part of the place, and walking through those rooms with Kate, her eyes animated, made my girlhood come alive for both of us.

For many years, I went back to Fort Wayne precisely because my life was so full of change and turmoil that the fantasy of being able to go back sustained me. The still point that my hometown represented, fixed in my stable childhood memories, was as comforting as a mouthful of chocolate. I don't go back as often as I used to now, simply because I no longer need to.

The life I imagined for myself, growing up in that house in my old neighborhood, was simpler and neater than the one I actually ended up living. Life was, I thought then, a straight, unobstructed road to the destinations I would choose, with pretty vistas and sunsets on the way. Guided by my parents' example, I believed that marriages always lasted and that even when parents fought, they always made up. I knew no one whose parents were divorced, and if there was a single lesson we were all meant to learn, it was the value of staying the course.

I had an amazingly uneventful, happy childhood. By the time I was in third grade, I knew I wanted to be a doctor. I went to high school where I wasn't the prettiest or the most popular but did just fine as the editor of the yearbook. I sailed on to college, where the road took one unexpected turn, and went right on to medical school where, in my last year, I married a young man I'd known since childhood. I was twenty-four and, while life hadn't left me completely unscathed, the road ahead still looked pretty straight and relatively uncomplicated. My husband and I shared a common background and were each ambitious and eager; our parents had long known each other socially. It looked, from the outside at least, like a perfect match. He was a lawyer, I was a doctor, and it seemed the world was pretty much ours for the asking. I had chosen pediatrics for my residency, and the two of us moved to Pittsburgh to start our adult lives and begin the "happily ever after" part. I was proud I'd managed to grow up without ever making an important wrong turn or a major mistake.

The next few years would change all that. First, my marriage fell apart after just five years and then, I decided to leave pediatrics for a specialty in ear, nose, and throat surgery, something I saw as another public admission that I didn't know where I was going or what I was doing. I castigated myself for every false step I took. But looking back, those years mark the start of my real "growing up," the beginning of the long haul that would bring me to where I am today. Errors in judgment, wrong choices, and failures as well as successes and triumphs altered my vision of the road I was on and changed who I was. Now, looking back, I see that the map of my life has all manner of turns and twists, potholes and mud, dead ends and—now and again—a sweep of open road. It is not the map I expected to end up looking at, growing up in Fort Wayne, Indiana, but it is mine. It is also a record of an uneven, sometimes circuitous journey that I share with many women, if not in the specific details, then in its broad outlines.

Take marriage, for example. In America today, almost one in two women will find themselves living lives and on a path very different from their girlhood dreams. Gather a group of women together and the statistical likelihood is that almost half of them have been divorced at least once. They find themselves not only trying to start their lives over but, often, raising children with little or no emotional or financial support. By contrast, in my mother's generation, a gathering of women for coffee and cake would have had nine married women for every divorcée. In my grandmother's lifetime, a woman would have been far more likely to be widowed than divorced.

It took me a very long time to stop apologizing to myself, to my parents, and to anyone who mattered about how uneven the roads I'd taken turned out to be.

I know better now.

Looking back at my life, I have taken a necessary journey that has made me a person of a richer fabric, if a bit ragged around the edges. I know now, as I didn't then, that the journey itself is every bit as important as where the road finally takes us. I guess that's why my childhood furniture still decorates the house I live in and why I still drive the same old car, the 1983 BMW that was, along with my oldest child and the clothes on my back, all I was able to retrieve from my second marriage. It is also the car I drove from Little Rock to San Francisco to start my life over. The 150,000 miles on its odometer are an important reminder of where I once found myself—broke, the single mother of two, starting over and clueless about how to do it—and where I am now.

In fact, I might not have been able to get where I am today if I hadn't gone to those other places first. And for that reason, I'm hanging on to that car for as long as I can. It is my own personal, self-bestowed merit badge.

Telling our stories is important, and as I tell mine, both who I am and where I've been become clearer, more defined. I can look at the map in my mind's eye and I can see the intersections where my life took a new turn. I can point to the places where I changed, the events and people that taught me the meaning of joy, the junctures where I felt the full burden of despair. What's not visible when you're on the road is clearer in retrospect. I can now see that the roads I managed not to take were blessings, along with a few I probably should have taken after all. The map, like the journey of life it details, is still a work in progress, with plenty of intersections ahead.

When we look closely at the maps of our lives, we realize that each intersection is different. Some are roads we have chosen, deliberately or unthinkingly, and some are pathways others have chosen for us. Still others are detours or blind alleys. And then there are the intersections we can ascribe only to something larger than ourselves, a cosmic force we may call by one of many names. The important point is that each of these intersections has something to teach us, to inform our growth.

I honestly believe that if you and I were to sit down together, it's likely that we would discover more things that we have in common than things that set us apart. First and foremost, there is the miraculous, complicated, and sometimes hugely annoying biological design we share. The miracle of childbearing apart, we live in bodies that remind us, on a daily and a monthly basis for roughly four decades, that life is cyclical, not linear. In very literal ways, we live in bodies that are ever-changing, never static, and I think the changing nature of our bodies has made us the more flexible and adaptable of the species. If we pay attention to it, the cyclical nature of our bodies teaches us to see ourselves as always evolving and changing; at forty, we are not the same women we were at twenty. At sixty, we are once again different. And that is as it should be.

It is only when we tell the stories of our lives—to our sisters and mothers, to our girlfriends over wine or coffee, to our husbands and lovers late at night, to our children—that the major and minor intersections that have brought us to where we are become clear, as if as we'd marked a road map with a thick yellow marker the way we used to underline our textbooks in high school. Telling our stories teaches us how the categories we use to talk about the events in our lives—this was a "good" choice, this a "bad" one—are far too simple to actually describe the impact any given moment in our lives has had on who we are. We grow as women and stretch our souls in good times and bad, and that is precisely what makes the journey, no matter how hard, a necessary one.

I'm telling my stories here in the hope that it will encourage you to tell your stories in turn. The stories women share can become a wellspring of inspiration, example, or solace for other women elsewhere. In sharing our stories, we can, within the circle of women, help each other define our strengths and make peace with our weaknesses. We can turn the community of women into an open classroom where we can benefit and learn from one another's experiences. By listening to one another, we can also help new generations of American women —our daughters, granddaughters, and even great-granddaughters—come of age.

In the circle of women, we see ourselves in a different light. Storytelling reminds us that change—some of it invited, some unchosen—is not only an inevitable part of life but a necessary one, and that staying the course is not the only lesson of value. Instead of beating ourselves up for what we did or didn't do, we need to try to see the journey we've taken as necessary, glean from it what value we can, and start scanning the horizon for new opportunities.

The necessary journeys I have taken have made me a stronger, more resilient, more confident woman than my young girl self, lying on her bed in that cozy house in Fort Wayne, ever dreamed of becoming. Of course, when young girls daydream about the future, they only dream of *what* they'll be, not *who* they'll be. It takes the journey to teach you that who you are is more important than anything else.

I hope you'll find something in each one of the stories that follow to take away for yourself. I believe firmly and strongly that, as women, we are all fellow travelers, and each of us has something of value to teach the other in the course of the journey that is life.

Blind Alleys

❧

BUT . . . THERE IS usually a "but." Life is filled with modifiers.

Not every part of the life journey we experience is necessary to our growth. Not every passage is a place of illumination.

Sometimes, life takes us where there is little or nothing of positive value to be learned. These are dark places of anguish, despair, and, sometimes, shame, where our faith in ourselves and the workings of the world is shaken to the core.

These black places are, usually, not those we have chosen for ourselves. They are blind alleys, experiences that set us back, leave the self raw and bruised, or scar our souls. But telling our stories is transformative: When we share our stories, what was a dark place of pain in one woman's experience can become a source of light and information for a listener.

I know this to be true.

This story is one I have told only a handful of people, intimates all, in almost three decades. It is not a story I originally intended to tell, and I think it may surprise some people that I've chosen to now. But when we turn inward to try to make sense of where we've been and who we have become, we need to look at those parts of our lives that have influenced and shaped us without enriching our spirits.

In the heartland of America, where I grew up, the harvest of the fields has always depended on the farmer's ability to separate the grain from the chaff. So, too, the spiritual bounty of the necessary journey requires that we learn how to separate the meaningful from the meaningless, the moments that shape our souls from the random acts that blind us to all except pain or despair or humiliation.

In word and thought, we outline and set the blind alley apart from all else we've experienced. By doing so, we light a flickering candle in the darkness.

By telling this story, I make sense of the senseless.

Only the act of putting it on these pages finally integrates a horrible moment into the necessary journey of my soul.

⌇∞⌇

In my sophomore year in college, I was raped by an intruder who found his way into what I thought then was a safe and secure world. I was nineteen. The room I shared with Sandy in the all-girls dormitory, McNutt, at Indiana University was the fourth door down the hall from the stairway that gave access to the building. The outside doors were supposed to be locked and usually were. Our room was small with bunk beds, and I slept on the bottom. The door had a bolted lock, but that night I'd left it ajar, as we often did, so that my roommate, who was studying calculus downstairs, could get in without using her key or waking me.

I was sound asleep and there is little that I remember about that night except that I woke up suddenly, a man on top of me, a knife in his hand. I don't remember very much else, not even his leaving nor my fleeing the dorm. I do know that someone found me, hours later, wandering the old part of campus in my nightgown, and brought me back to my room. I have no idea who that someone was or what, if anything, I said to explain myself.

I did what no rape victim should ever do. I cleaned

myself up, told no one, and pretended that nothing had happened to me. What was I thinking? Probably this: If I didn't tell and didn't confront it, I would stay the same young woman I'd been before.

But I wasn't the same. Something *had* happened to me. My world had suddenly turned unsafe. I was too young and not introspective enough to know that things put in shallow graves don't stay put.

My grades plummeted that spring and I floated through my daily life unmoored and, looking back, totally isolated by my decision to deny the rape. Was it really a decision? You couldn't call it that, not when I was nineteen. I did what I thought would hold my life together. And by keeping my silence, I made the same mistake many women, young and old alike, continue to make today, with devastasting results.

My depression worsened and, at the semester's end, I told my parents I thought I needed to take a year off before tackling junior year. I offered no explanations. Perhaps I'd just travel, I ventured. A girl I knew from school was going to take a year off; maybe I'd tag along. They were, not surprisingly, stunned and said "no." As a family, they believed in the value of my learning to stay the course.

By shutting my parents out, I denied myself the possibility of a safe haven and cut off whatever help they might have given me. Left in the dark, they had no way of gauging how depressed I really was. When I suggested that I might find someone to talk to, my father, concerned about my chances of being accepted into medical school after being treated for depression, suggested instead that we take a weekend in Chicago. (In retrospect, it's easy to fault my dad on this, but I'd given him no reason to assume that anything of importance had happened to me. My father was probably right about medical school: In the 1970s, depression was not something anyone in a position of responsibility confessed to. Confessing cost Missouri Senator Thomas Eagleton the nomination for vice president. Even close to thirty years later, when the spouse of an elected official, Tipper Gore, made her treatment for depression public, it was considered newsworthy.)

The weekend in Chicago with my father, while fun and distracting, changed nothing.

I spent the summer eating, gaining forty pounds in the process. Listening to music. Being quiet. I'd get in the car and drive to my old neighborhood and climb the giant fir tree I'd played in as a child. Sitting high up in its branches, the landscape spread out before me, made me feel calm and safe. I still had told no one. Perhaps, by then, I had managed to convince myself it had never happened, but I'm not sure.

The summer ended and, somehow, life went on. I managed to push the thought of what had happened to me further and further from view so that it had, I thought, actually disappeared. I don't think, in my mind, that I had given what happened a name, and all these years later, even writing the words "rape" and "sexual assault" are still difficult. There was safety in not thinking, not remembering. My grades went back to being what they'd been. "It" was behind me, except for the weight I'd gained.

(Those extra pounds, which stayed on right through medical school, were the only outward sign of what was wrong within. They were, I think, a kind of armor as well as an unconscious statement of how I really felt about myself.)

I'd built only the flimsiest of boats—really more like a leaf floating on the surface of a river—to keep myself afloat.

Two years later, during Thanksgiving vacation of my senior year, the most innocent of comments ended my self-imposed exile. I was standing in the kitchen with my parents, having a drink before the holiday feast. At this point, my applications to medical school were in and my interviews complete, but I was understandably nervous about the stiff competition. My father remarked about how good my grades were, except for that one spring semester. Unspoken was the thought that those low grades, in important courses, might well keep me from getting in and becoming a doctor.

Unthinking, tears welling up and then spilling over, I blurted out that I had been raped. My parents' pain was palpable. They stood frozen, their faces stricken. The source of their pain, I now realize all these years later, as a parent myself, was not simply the horror of what had happened but that they hadn't been able to protect me from it. By shutting them out for two years, I had also, unwittingly, taken away their opportunity to help me heal.

My secret was, finally, out.

꙯

But it wasn't really. I didn't go into therapy or seek other help then. Instead, wrongly, I continued to let the flow of everyday life—the progression of days and months, waking and sleeping, going to classes, getting into medical school, and finally, graduating—carry me farther and farther from that awful night.

But platitudes aside, time only scabs over our wounds. It does not heal them.

What I did to myself compounded what had been done to me. By not confiding in anyone, I allowed myself to feel responsibile and guilty for something that had nothing to do with me or who I was. It wasn't clear to me, then, that had my door been bolted, the rapist would have simply continued down the hallways, checking for an open door. And what happened to me might have happened to another sleeping girl instead.

And she would have been no more accountable, no more to blame, for what happened than I was.

But by keeping my silence, I let what had happened to me became a reflection of me. I let myself be shamed by the experience, turning my disgust at the experience into disgust at myself. Shame insinuates itself into a woman's spirit, twisting and turning like a snake, half-hidden by grasses, in search of prey. I became timid. I felt unworthy. Overweight, I hated how I looked.

Most important, I became afraid. The world had turned dangerous and, in small ways and large, I became a fearful young woman, made uncomfortable by someone walking behind me, even on a crowded sidewalk in broad daylight. To this day, when I sit in a restaurant, I sit with my back to the wall so I can see who is coming toward me. My relationship to men shifted in subtle but meaningful ways. I sought out men who were nice to me on the surface, who validated my chipped-away sense of self. I cowered when they raised their voices, and learned to distance myself emotionally whenever the going got rough. I could not permit them ever to be angry and, when they were, I drifted away in response.

I went on to succeed at many things and, despite what had happened, to grow and change. The rape remained walled off, but because I hadn't confronted what had happened to me, it cast a dark shadow.

It wasn't until my life truly fell apart years later that I actually sought the help I needed.

The lesson in this experience for me? There isn't one, really. This blind alley simply made the necessary part of my journey just that much harder. There's no silver lining when a woman is left violated and trembling. My life would have been just fine, thank you very much, had this not happened.

∞

But . . . There is a lesson to be drawn from the telling. While we can't prevent bad things from happening to us or our daughters or our sisters or our friends, what we can do is seek the help we need when an act of violence touches our lives.

If we cannot talk to our parents or our sisters or our husbands or our friends, then we must take it upon ourselves to find someone we can talk to. That someone can be a minister or priest, a doctor, a therapist, a counselor, or a volunteer at a crisis center. We must break the silence. As mothers, we must tell our daughters again and again that we are always there for them and that, no matter what takes place in a sometimes dangerous world, we will love them and stand by them without questioning. We need to examine whatever prejudices we hold to make sure that if, God forbid, something does happen to any girl or woman we care about, our words are true, consistent, and uncritical.

While we can't entirely prevent acts of violence, we can exert control over the aftermath of any crisis. We have it in our power to stop our bad experiences from taking over our lives. We can work together to insure that when a woman is victimized, the damage done is not compounded by either the woman herself or society at large. We can, through the intervention of professionals, friends, and loved ones, prevent the blind alley from leading us into a crisis of self-doubt and self-abuse.

Silence only makes a place of darkness darker.

According to recent statistics, depending on the study consulted, as many as one in five but certainly no fewer than one in eight women in the United States over the age of twelve will, in their lifetimes, be the victim or the intended victim of rape or sexual assault. These numbers are staggering, whether you accept the one in five—a full 20 percent—or the lower number, one in eight. (In 1992 one in eight translated into 12.1 million American women. What more needs to be said?)

If you have been lucky enough not to have been the target of sexual assault and think you know no one who has been, the likelihood is that you are wrong. Most probably, the victim has simply kept her silence.

A study on rape released almost eight years ago, prepared jointly by the National Victim Center in Virginia and the Crime Victims Research and Treatment Center in South Carolina, reveals the social truths behind the statistics. Although we tend to think of rape as a crime perpetrated upon a victim by a stranger as it was in my case, in fact these constitute only 25 percent of the rape cases reported. In 75 percent of the cases of these violent acts, the assailant is known to the victim.

Most telling, perhaps, is what the study found about the concerns of the rape victim. Chief among these were not, as you might think, fear of pregnancy or disease but, instead, the reaction of friends and family to the knowledge of the assault; fear that people would blame or consider her responsible for what had happened; the humiliation of her name being made public. Shame is still an important consequence of rape.

We need, as women, to gather ourselves in a circle around the victimized, the assaulted, the beaten among us, much as the pioneers circled their wagons to protect their own as they crossed the landscape of America in search of their futures. We need to stop reassuring ourselves that it could *never* happen to us or anyone we know by distancing ourselves from the women to whom it has happened, by imagining that they are somehow responsible for the acts forced upon them.

Whether it's one in five or one in eight isn't the point. As an exercise, we should go anywhere where girls and women congregate—in stores, at laundromats, in playgrounds, churches, or anywhere else—and we should look at the faces before us, young and old, and do a count. If there are sixteen girls in a playground, then it is likely that at least two of them will, in their lifetimes, become victims. The numbers tell us that it can happen to any one of us, our daughters, our sisters, our friends, our colleagues, our neighbors.

We need to let go of the social stigmas that prevent women from speaking up, and put the blame where it belongs: on the assailant.

We need to tell our stories and to listen to each other with open minds and hearts so that we can allow the circle of women to aid in the process of healing. It is less difficult to recognize the blind alley in company; it is less daunting to get on with the business of the necessary journey at hand when we don't feel quite so alone.

By putting these words on the pages you're reading, I have both closed the door on a night of horror almost three decades ago and opened it at the same time. I now see the terrible confusion of my younger self with clarity and understand how, by denying the assault on both my body and spirit, I allowed the hurt and pain within me to manifest themselves in my life in unproductive and unnecessary ways.

Finally, by telling this story, I am at last able to put what happened that night to good use.

Inspirations

∽

FROM A VERY young age, I dreamed of becoming a doctor.

As children, we all dream of our futures and, for some of us, the dreams of childhood directly and clearly form the path we will take into the world. Unlike many girls, then or now, I did not dream alone. As the first-born in my family, medicine was practically ordained to be part of my future from birth: The first two years that I occupied center stage in the family, before my three siblings were born, convinced my father that I had the stuff to follow in his and his father's footsteps, physicians both. Amazingly, the fact that I was a daughter seems not to have made a difference to him, although it would to the world and to me. It's a family joke that my father programmed me to be a doctor, proof that family jokes often contain more than a little bit of truth.

As children, adolescents, and later, women, our dreams awaken us to possibility. By imagining something beyond the reality of "now"—whether it is the now of girlhood or of womanhood—we give ourselves permission to grow and change, and to take on new aspects of self. We take the first step toward believing in ourselves by dreaming, and what we dream is less important than the act of dreaming itself.

Understanding what we can learn from others is the first step toward making our dreams come true. While the solitary dreamer has the burden of inventing herself, those of us with strong role models—whether they are parents, teachers, or bosses—need to learn a different lesson entirely, taking from our mentors what is useful and productive for us and making it our own, and letting go of what we don't need.

Giving voice to our selves takes time and work. There are no shortcuts.

Medicine was a part of my childhood even though my father's respect for the doctor-patient privilege was such that we never heard about his cases. By the time I was in kindergarten, my father took me on his Sunday morning rounds. Because in those days children weren't allowed beyond the first floor of a hospitals (they were thought to be germ-carriers and thus a risk to the patients), I spent my time in the doctors' lounge, drinking chocolate milk, and eating chocolate-covered graham crackers. But just being there made me feel important and a part of my father's world, and perhaps that is all a young child needs to fuel her dreams.

My earliest memories are of my father rushing out of our house, his medical bag in hand, toward the busy state highway just down the street from us. It was a dangerous intersection and, hearing the awful sound of screeching brakes and metal hitting metal, he'd be out the door, heading to the accident to offer help. By the time I was ten, I was brave enough to run down the hill with him and look on from a distance, while my mother called an ambulance.

I got my first real taste of the medical world the summer between my junior and senior years in high school. I got a job as an assistant to the respiratory therapists in our local hospital, and my experience that summer both tested and confirmed my commitment to medicine. It wasn't a job a youngster could land now in the world of malpractice and corporate hospitals, but, in those days in Fort Wayne, being a hard worker, well-mannered, and the daughter of a respected doctor was enough. I gave breathing treatments to patients and delivered supplies to the nurses' stations. What I did was simple enough that I could do the patients no harm. The patients I connected with were usually the very old (I guess my young face was meant to cheer them up) or teenagers like myself. I became friends with a number of them, one of them a girl around thirteen or fourteen, a few years younger than I was. I didn't know what was wrong with her and, to this day, I don't know for sure.

In that beeperless and cellular-free world, doctors were called over pages. Occasionally, I heard an emergency code blare—"Dr. Blue" meant a life-and-death emergency and "Dr. Red" meant there was a fire somewhere in the hospital—but most of the summer days passed without incident. When I heard a "Dr. Blue" code, I knew to rush the cart of supplies as quickly as possible to the room number called, but I'd always been sent away without seeing anything.

One morning, a "Dr. Blue" came over the loudspeaker. I raced to the room, not even registering that it was the room of my young friend, whom I'd seen just a few hours before. I was the first person there, and I swung the door open. There was blood everywhere and soon the room filled with doctors and nurses. I pressed myself hard against the wall and stood there, paralyzed. I had no idea the human body contained so much blood.

The team worked frantically to save her as I watched my friend bleed to death.

No one noticed me as the fast pace of lifesaving gave way to the official routines of declaring the time of death, inventorying supplies, and then cleaning the hospital room. I stood stock-still, my back against the wall. Tears streamed down my face but I was so numbed that I didn't even know I was crying. Finally, one of the doctors, Dr. Leming, an old friend of my parents, took me by the hand and led me out of there. He even called my mother to have me picked up and taken home.

I was devastated, and the raw physical details of her death—the blood everywhere, the chest bone cracked open, the frantic efforts of the team to stop the bleeding—left me with vivid images I couldn't get out of my head. I was a high school kid, after all—not even a college student, much less a medical student or a resident. The awful unfairness of a girl so young dying so horribly, alone in a hospital room, shook me to the core. Where was God in all of this? It was the first time, though not the last, that my Sunday school faith had been tested. I couldn't sleep, the vision still fresh and awful, and, the next day my mother tried to tell me that medicine wasn't the only path out there if I wasn't cut out for it. Meaning only to comfort, she reminded me that perhaps this wasn't for me and that I didn't *have* to be a doctor. I don't remember the exchange but my mother does: Hours later, I marched into the kitchen and replied, curtly and rudely, "Don't ever say that to me again."

Of course, I wasn't talking back to just my mother.

❧

I went back to work at the hospital and later that summer there was another Code Blue, this time to the emergency room. I ran, and there, on a gurney, lay a two-year-old girl. In the confusion, I heard the sobs of the mother, the fast staccato of the nurses' questions, the fact that the child's airway was blocked. The emergency room doctor tried, without success, to get a tube down the toddler's throat, and I watched, horrified, as her color changed from ashen to mottled sky blue to steel blue in moments. They called for an ear, nose, and throat surgeon to perform an emergency tracheotomy.

The doors between the emergency room and the hospital's main corridors swung open, and the atmosphere changed with the doctor's presence. He called for a size-two tracheotomy tube. His hands sure and swift, he incised the child's neck and inserted the tube in less than a minute. As I watched, her skin began to glow with life, turning from blue to pink.

The doctor was my father and I watched as he saved a life. It was an extraordinary moment.

The word "inspire" means to breathe air or life into, and that, of course, is precisely what I watched my father do. But I, too, was changed by those events I witnessed; I knew with absolute certainty what I wanted to do with my life. My vision was focused and my father became my first professional role model. But in the end, my father's example was secondary to something far more important: his and my mother's faith in my abilities. That faith provided me with the unwavering support I needed to make my way in the male world of medicine.

We need, in the community of women, to make it our business to insure that every girl and boy in America has at least one adult who believes in her or him without reservation.

∞

Not long ago, I asked a very succcessful female producer at ABC News whom she considered a role model or mentor in her professional life. After a pause, she answered: "I've never had one." Her answer is, I think, a common one for the women now in their forties and fifties, professional women of my generation, who imagined their futures without the benefit of a role model. While I was clearly blessed to have my father as my personal one-man marching band, in order to establish my own female identity as a doctor, I still had to find my own way. I chose pediatrics initially precisely because he wasn't a pediatrician and, perhaps, because the specialty—which stresses nurturance—was and is female-friendly medicine. In my second year of residency, when it became clear to me that pediatrics would not hold my interest but that my father's specialty—ear, nose, and throat surgery—would, I made plans and switched without ever telling him or asking his advice. It was a small but necessary rebellion: To become Dr. Nancy Snyderman, I had to stop being, professionally at least, Dr. Sanford Snyderman's daughter.

Even with the best role models serving as examples—whether they are our parents or not—one part of the journey is always solitary.

In medical school and during my residency, the lack of female role models had an odd, unexpected benefit. Because my womanhood prevented me from following the examples of my male teachers and surgeons in a literal way, I was able to take bits and pieces—techniques, manner, understanding—from each of them to define myself as the best surgeon I could become. They, in turn, rewarded me for my hard work. To become the best doctor I could be, I turned to female examples—my mother, the nurses in the hospital—who taught me the importance of talking and touching, all the things that our culture sees as essentially "feminine" in nature. Nurturance comes easily to women, as does the habit of mind and spirit to emphasize relationship and connection, and both were important strengths for me to draw on as a healer and a teacher.

Girls and young women today are surrounded by many more sources of female inspiration than I was as a girl, dreaming on my bed in Fort Wayne. Over the last forty years, women have become familiar, if hardly ubiquitous, presences in almost every field of endeavor in America. The statistics appear to be encouraging, although they convey something less than a level playing field for women and men. In 1960 only 5.5 percent of American doctors were female; by 1990 the percentage was 25.5 percent. Astonishingly, by the mid-1990s, 45 percent of all medical students were women. Fewer than one percent of dentists were women in 1960; in 1990 15.4 percent were women. In dental hygiene and physical therapy, ancillary areas of medicine requiring less education and costly training, women represented 99 percent and 75 percent of the respective fields. In other fields, 26 percent of the nation's lawyers are now women, while women occupy 40 percent of all management positions in business.

But we all know that there is still a long way to go. Women still make 76 cents for every dollar earned by men in similar positions. Evidence of the glass ceiling is everywhere and is particularly marked in certain fields, such as business and medicine, fields that are high-paying, high-status, and drive public policy.

Young girls today have visible female role models which my generation, for the most part, lacked. (As girls, we had to summon up the rare heroine, the singular Marie Curie, Amelia Earhart, or Margaret Mead.) Nevertheless, dreaming the dream and holding on to it hasn't gotten any easier, and it's still much harder for girls than it is for their male counterparts.

That is disturbing news.

A landmark study first commissioned by the American Association of University Women in 1991 and revised as recently as two years ago, showed that while elementary-school-aged girls and boys feel almost equally confident in their abilities to do things, girls begin to slip in middle school. By the time girls go to high school, roughly half of them have already lost that confidence. More significantly, when girls and boys have trouble with math and science, they interpret their difficulties in very different and telling ways. Boys discount the value of the subject, while girls blame their intelligence (or lack of it) and thus internalize their failures.

Doesn't this sound familiar? Society conditions a female to be a good, responsible girl, who is also modest and reticent about her accomplishments. (A driven man is ambitious; a driven woman is aggressive and, sometimes, worse.) Talk to a successful woman and she'll tell you how "lucky" she's been. Talk to a successful man and he'll tell you how hard he's worked to get where he is. In my experience, success comes from a combination of hard work and opportunity, a word I prefer to "luck." I've worked hard and, yes, I have tried to capitalize on every opportunity that came my way.

In my generation, as women went out into the workplace in record numbers and established a female beachhead in many professions, we did so without the benefit of the company of women. In fact, to blend into the male world, we had to draw as little attention to our femaleness as possible. All of us were careful to put on what could only be described as a female version of a man's suit—inside and out—and to act accordingly.

If we want to keep our girls dreaming, the moment has come to let our femaleness begin to show. In search of equality, we have gotten used to saying, whenever one of our number accomplishes anything, that being a woman has "nothing" to do with the accomplishment. This disclaimer—which has the important and damaging side effect of having us deny our selfhood in the same moment that we accept society's praise—isn't healthy for us or the next generation of women. Practically speaking, the disclaimer serves to disarm the criticism we've come to expect from society. "Nothing to do with being a woman" is really shorthand for "I didn't use my femininity 'unfairly,'" "I didn't sleep my way to the top," "I'm not just a token appointment or a public relations stunt," or "I earned this fair and square." We succeed at life because of who we are, and who we are is indistinguishable from our femaleness.

To keep our girls dreaming, we must all work together or all the role models in the world won't make a difference. For those of us forging new paths in the outside world, we must make it our business to stop sounding as though being a woman is an impediment we need to deny or a problem we must manage. For those of us who have chosen to follow the paths of homemaker and mother, we must stop acting as though the word "woman" belongs to us alone, and insinuating that those making different choices are not really "women" at all.

Our being women has everything to do with everything we do. Our selfhood and our womanhood are indistinguishable. As women, we bring unique qualities to every venture in our lives—from supervising homework to starting a new business, from litigating or negotiating a merger to writing a book or sewing sutures or managing a household—which are tied to the "feminine" aspects of our nature, to our changing bodies, to the ways we are markedly different from the male of the human species.

I can say with certainty that I am a different doctor than I would have been had I been born a man. If I had chosen to be a lawyer, my womanhood would have made me a different lawyer than if I had been born a man. If I'd been a landscape architect or a baker, then, too, my femaleness would have been part and parcel of my work.

And I say it without apology. We need to tell this simple truth to our girls and find ways of celebrating those differences in each and every one of us that distinguish us from men.

Perhaps when we have learned to say that what we have accomplished has everything to do with who we are as people *and* women, then perhaps, we will finally see ourselves wholly and with a new perspective. Perhaps, then, our girls will stop starting to fail when their bodies begin to cross the line between childhood and womanhood. When we've stopped pretending that being a woman doesn't matter, we will be able, as women, to draw on each other—no matter what we do in the world —for strength and inspiration. This is important not simply for girls but for all women who, at different points in the journey, need to be able to change their minds about where they are going, and need the support of the community of women to get there.

And we need to remember that our dreams are the seeds of the future at every stage of our lives.

Mirror Images

∞

THE FIRST BEND in the road chosen took me by surprise. Actually, it was less like a bend than a deep rut through which I stumbled, bruised and bleeding more than a little.

Looking back, I realize that while deciding what I wanted to be—a doctor—was easier for me than it is for many women, finding the self inside the white coat was much, much more difficult. Learning to like and feel comfortable with myself was harder still, and took even longer.

As young adults, we venture out into the world, away from the familiar settings and definitions of our girlhood. Guided only by our dreams, we begin the journey toward selfhood. For many of us, this part of the path is shaped by the experiences of our adolescence, when we've managed to pick up all sorts of emotional baggage that doesn't make the going any easier.

Sometimes, as I did, we look to find our selves in the wrong places.

∞

The first adult decision I made was to get married at the age of twenty-four, after I finished medical school. It was also the first decision I had ever made without my father's approval and, at the time, I honestly believed that my choice marked a turning point in a newfound, more confident independence.

I married for love in more ways than one. I had known the man I married since kindergarten, and had gone to grade school, junior high, and high school with him. Our parents had known each other for many years, and he'd grown up in a beautiful two-story brick house, right near mine, across the street from the big fir tree. We each went off to different colleges and, then, the summer between our first and second years in graduate school (he was in law school while I was in medical school), we suddenly saw each other with new eyes. He was smart, well-read, and witty, and I loved the challenge of talking to him, being with him. He was sexy and ambitious and fun.

Despite all of my accomplishments, I was terribly insecure, unhappy with my looks, but being loved by him made me feel better about myself. Marriage was, I thought, a logical step.

My father disagreed. He argued that we were both too young and that my residency—the most self-centered and time-consuming part of a young doctor's training—would get in the way. I was headstrong enough to defy my father although, in retrospect, it's clear that I hadn't yet become truly independent. True independence would take me years to achieve.

The details of the wedding itself should have clued me into what was really happening, but I didn't know enough to pay attention. We took my father's counsel and settled on a week-long trip to London as a wedding gift, rather than a big wedding and reception, which he'd argued were just a waste of money. The little girl in me still thought that Daddy was always right, and I think that set the tone of the marriage from the start. The wedding itself was a rather haphazard affair, not helped by the fact that the evening we'd chosen for our nuptials was the night of the Big Ten finals.

If you know anything about Indiana, you know

that basketball rules. As luck would have it, the game that night was Indiana and Michigan, and the priest was from Michigan. In full consideration of the relative importance of events, we postponed the ceremony until after the game was over. (I have a vague recollection that Michigan won but I may be wrong about that.) The rebel in me didn't want a dress with flounces and lace and, besides, I still didn't feel pretty enough to splurge, so I wore something I'd borrowed from my mother, a cream-colored dress and jacket that, if the photographs tell the truth, were less than flattering. While we laughed about how offbeat and funky the wedding was, in retro-spect, I see that what was missing was commitment.

I don't think I spent a moment thinking about what marriage really meant. My parents' marriage was a happy one and, since I was still seeing them through a daughter's eyes, I didn't even begin to fathom what com-bination of love, patience, and sacrifice they'd managed to summon to make it work. I didn't know anyone who had been divorced, and it never occurred to me that the model of my parents' marriage, or any marriage, for that matter, in the small world we'd both grown up in— tra-ditional marriages with a stay-at-home wife—would be no help to us, the young doctor and lawyer, as we tried to find our way.

The honeymoon over, we settled down to real life in Pittsburgh, on what would prove to be a collision course with one another. I had gotten married but my real commitment was to medicine, one which intensified when, after two years, I switched my residency from pediatrics to, first, general surgery and then to ear, nose, and throat surgery, thereby lengthening my time of train-ing. My husband spent more and more time alone as I spent more and more time at the hospital. I was on call three days a week, working and staying up twenty-four hours. Ambitious and excited by medicine, I honestly didn't see why I should go home for dinner if I could first assist on a surgery that started at eight p.m. Nothing in my husband's childhood had prepared him for living with a wife who wasn't on call for him.

I wrapped medicine around me like a warm, pro-tective blanket. Working with patients opened up a new world where my common sense, my compassion, and my knowledge combined to really let me shine at something. Within the hospital walls where the sick needed help, I discovered my talents and a self-confidence that eluded me elsewhere. Inside the white coat, I was somebody: Dr. Nancy Snyderman. The white coat off, I was a self-conscious young woman who was failing at her marriage.

My husband felt increasingly left out (he was) and depressed. He wanted more of a wife, not to mention more of a life. Neither of us was capable of giving an inch, and the ways in which we connected to each other became darker, full of shadows. Unable to budge me, he began to badger me in self-defense. And the more frustrated he became, the more I withdrew into my ambition and my work, my attention focused on the one place in my life where I actually felt good, even terrific, about myself. He was angry at what he perceived as my betrayal and, in the end, became accusatory. It was a dark time.

And so, disappointed and hurt, I ended it. It seemed simple on the surface: We separated almost immediately after five years of marriage and divorced, leaving with the belongings we brought into the union. I returned the engagement ring, which had belonged to his grandmother, but kept the beautiful piece of French luggage my parents had given us as a wedding gift. It was civilized, as these things go, but hugely painful.

My sense of personal failure was enormous and a source of great embarrassment: I'd gotten an F in the first truly adult thing I'd tried and everyone—family, friends, even casual acquaintances—knew it. And after I moved from Pittsburgh, I just casually edited it out of my personal history, a five-year stretch no one needed to know about. Once again, I turned away from what I needed to look at—that inner self, eager for validation and hungry for love—which was so markedly different from the exterior I allowed the world to see, the ambitious and successful young doctor.

All that meant was that I didn't learn what I needed to be able to choose a different path the next time. Looking away pretty much insured that I would end up making another bad choice.

I did. But the next time, I would take a much harder fall.

⁓

Twenty years later, with the benefits of hindsight and other peoples' insights, it's not so hard to understand what was happening to me. Lack of self-esteem is a problem for thousands upon thousands of girls and young women in a society that is not user-friendly to young women, as Dr. Mary Pipher's book, *Reviving Ophelia*—which should be required reading for life— makes brillantly, terribly, clear. When I was in college, a roommate made me a cross-stitched sampler that reads, "I know I'm efficient. Tell me I'm beautiful," and maybe that goes to the heart of the matter. Inside the doctor's white coat was an overweight, self-conscious young woman who, when she looked in the mirror, saw the reflection of someone who failed the impossible standards of high school.

Before my forties—which have been a personal time of flowering—the last time I had genuinely liked the way I looked was in ninth grade. Like the majority of girls, I'd never been pretty enough to be homecoming queen or popular enough to sit on the court. I didn't shine at the things that made you part of the much-envied "in" crowd in high school, and I can still remember how I felt like an outsider just talking to the girls who were part of that popular group (I knew them from summers at the local country club). The minute I walked up, they would change their conversation. I worked hard at academics, the goals of college and medical school before me, but watched the cool kids and the cheerleaders from the stands.

The assault I suffered in college only made everything I already felt about myself worse. My weight was both a source of pain and my armor at once and, by the time I got to medical school, I had become my own worst enemy, making sure I excluded myself before anyone excluded me. At 180 pounds, I was so self-conscious about how I looked that, rather than walk through the main doors of the amphitheater where lectures were given, I slipped through doors at the top, so that no one could see me.

Like many women, I looked to marriage and a man not only to assuage my loneliness but to make me whole.

But only in fantasy can someone bestow you with a self.

∞

The continuing problems I had with self-esteem are, tragically, rather ordinary, affecting large numbers of American girls and young women. Older women who find themselves at a crossroads in their lives—during a divorce, for example, or after being fired from a job—often discover, in the center of their souls where their self-reliance ought be, an unhappy teenage girl. My experience isn't all that unusual; I've sat and talked with many women—outwardly successful and gifted professionals—who have spent years repairing their inner selves.

It is sobering to observe that, despite the comparative abundance of female role models that my generation of women lacked—strong women of talent whose success and fulfillment do not depend on their looks—not much has changed since I was a teenager, surrounded by images of the blond, thin, blue-eyed beauty queen I'd never be. In fact, things are now even worse, in a culture where, in Dr. Pipher's words, "Beauty is the defining characteristic for American women. It's the necessary and often sufficient condition for social success." Of all the dismaying facts Dr. Pipher reveals in *Reviving Ophelia*, perhaps none is as terrible as her admission that in all the years that she has been a therapist, she has "yet to meet one girl who likes her body." (She recounts, too, that when she speaks to classes, she invites women in the audience who feel good about their bodies to come forward afterward to share their stories. No one ever does.)

What this translates into are distressing statistics: According to Dr. Pipher, one in five young women in America has an eating disorder.

One in five. And while it is true that this number has garnered publicity and attention, partly because of Dr. Pipher's work, it is one that still should galvanize each and every one of us into action. (Estimates on how many young women suffer from eating disorders vary. According to the National Women's Health Information Center, approximately one percent of adolescent girls develop bulimia nervosa. But a 1990 study undertaken by the National association of Anorexia Nervosa and associated Disorders found that 11 percent of young people, in high school (both male and female) suffered from an eating disorder. The Association points out that since the study did not include early adolescent populations, a large group in which eating disorders are reported was not covered. Most important, the rate of cure is only 50 percent.)

There is no statistic for the number of unhappy but still functioning women the culture of beauty has produced. And we need to count among them the beautiful women who have been equally, if differently, stigmatized by cultural assumptions.

As mothers, aunts, grandmothers, sisters, and girlfriends, we need to take responsibility for helping each other cultivate the garden of the female self. We need to remind each other and our children that personal growth is a process and that we can learn equally from our failures and our successes. We need to banish the word "perfect" from our vocabularies.

We need to shout from the rooftops that self-worth comes from within—not from having blond hair or a perky figure—and that we are made whole, competent, and strong by discovering our talents and choosing our own paths. We grow from learning how to choose wisely and well. As role models, we must rid ourselves of our own girlhood tics based in the culture of beauty. We have to realize that when we judge ourselves by our looks alone—the thinness of our thighs or, inversely, the wrinkles around our eyes—we too are sending our daughters a message.

We need to support each other in the unlearning.

We must understand that no one can make us whole when we feel broken except ourselves. We need to stop telling the stories of the princes who can transform our lives and repair our sense of self simply by their presence. Until we make ourselves whole, true partnership will continue to elude us, and only in true partnership will we find the "true" love the fairy tales have encouraged us to seek. We become ourselves only by doing the work of living with open eyes, without looking away as I did for so many years. To see ourselves clearly, we need to see ourselves truly, reminding each other that asking for help is a sign of strength, not weakness.

We need to celebrate our womanhood, and look at our bodies not through the eyes of a Hollywood talent agent or an adolescent boy but with understanding. We are, biologically, the most complex members of the human species, artfully designed to bear and nuture the race. Our curves, the proportion of fat on our bodies, and even the cycles of hormones that make us creatures of change are part of a cosmic design.

When we look in the mirror, we need to judge the beauty of our bodies by how we feel living in them, not by whether our bellies are concave or our noses straight.

Finally, in the circle of women, we need to recognize that, if we want the young women who will forge their way in the next century and millennium to feel better about themselves, then we must take on the task of changing how our society sees and judges women. We need to speak up about what really matters wherever we find ourselves—at home, in school yards and playgrounds, in classrooms and offices, in churches and communities—and make our voices heard. We owe it to ourselves and the women of the future.

A Change of Direction

∞

THE SIMPLE "I" we use to describe ourselves doesn't begin to tell the truth. We all need it as a starting place: "I" sets us apart, and distinguishes us from "we" and "ours" and "you" and "yours." It is how, as children, we cast our first sentences and separate ourselves from the others—mothers, fathers, sisters, brothers—who make up our little worlds. It is the pronoun that lets us tell the first stories in which we have the starring roles. "I" is, grammatically, singular, but the grammar belies the complexity of each and every one of us.

The self we describe with the shorthand "I" is more like a mirrored mosaic than anything else, reflecting not just where we are but where we've been and where we dream of going. Every role we've played in life—whether that of daughter, lover, friend, mother, laundry-folder, caregiver, wrapper of gifts, gardener, doctor, lawyer, pilot, cook—finds its expression in the self. Like the bodies we inhabit, variable and never static—changing with the moon, and then decade by decade—our female selves are everchanging, ever evolving. Within the self, the pronoun "I" takes in the girls we were, the young women we became, the women we hope to be in the future.

The journey that is life offers each of us myriad opportunities to take on and express new aspects of self, and continues to, until we take our last breath. And when it doesn't, it's up to us to imagine the opportunity we need, and to work to make it happen. Invariably, the bigger we dream, the farther the dream can take us.

I didn't dream my career in television as a girl or even as a young woman, but I knew enough to recognize a good thing when I saw one. And to hang on to it.

∽

My first appearance on television, when I was an otolaryngology resident on the pediatric ear, nose, and throat rotation at the University of Pittsburgh, happened pretty much by accident. A television show was doing a report on whether tonsillectomies were being performed too often in America, and the show's producers hoped to have the chief of surgery expound on the question. As luck would have it, he had absolutely no interest in being interviewed and he designated me as his fill-in .

I hesitated a second, and blurted out that perhaps I didn't know enough to be interviewed. He responded quickly; if I wasn't knowledgeable enough to be on television, maybe then I shouldn't be graduating.

That settled it, and I found myself in the unlikely situation—dressed in my resident's greens, with no makeup, and a nanosecond of preparation in the dingy hallway outside of the operating room—of being the expert opinion. Afterward, the producer asked if I'd ever done television before. I said I hadn't, and he answered that I ought to think about it.

And so I did.

It didn't take long before the KDKA morning show and other stations in Pittsburgh were calling the young Dr. Snyderman to report on everything from swimmer's ear to how to avoid having a heart attack when shoveling snow—a hot topic, as you might imagine, in snowbound Pittsburgh. Television, then as now, allowed me to be a medical generalist, and I loved it. The pay? None, except a tape of the broadcast, which they were happy to provide.

But it wasn't about money. Being on television was fun, and I liked the work for any number of reasons. Yes, it made me feel important and less insecure about myself, but I also thought I was doing something valuable: getting the information out there. Television was definitely something I wanted to try in my life and, frankly, I didn't see why I couldn't.

I didn't know enough about television to realize how hard it could be or how unlikely it was that I'd actually succeed at it. I didn't know enough to stop trying, and there was no one around to tell me how hopeless it was, the way there might have been in a more cosmopolitan environment—and a larger television market —like Chicago or Boston. I didn't prepare by taking acting or elocution lessons; I simply figured being a doctor was enough.

And so, when I moved to Little Rock after my residency, I took my stash of Pittsburgh videotapes, those old $3/4$-inch reels, with me, and I started asking around. As luck would have it, a medical student on my service was married to one of the local anchors, and the anchor arranged for me to have an interview at the local NBC affiliate. (She also introduced me to the man who would become my second husband, but that's another story entirely and *not* her fault.) The NBC affiliate was distinctly underwhelmed, and my interview went nowhere. They even managed to misplace the tapes I'd loaned them. Nothing lost, nothing gained; I had a day job, after all.

I walked the few blocks to the ABC station, asked for the news director, and, given that it was Little Rock, actually got him. My pitch went like this: There weren't any doctor-reporters on the air in town, and there should be. It was an important city, after all. Once that was agreed, I was the perfect fit. I had the right medical credentials and television experience. I even had tapes to prove it.

Someone I'd run into in Pittsburgh, a psychologist who did on-air occasionally, had once offered the advice that I should ask for twice the union rate while negotiating. Armed with that bit of information—mind you, the only information I had—when the boss asked me what I wanted, I was filled with confidence. "Two times union rate," I replied firmly. There was a slight pause and then he leaned across the table, smiled, and said, slowly and without even a touch of irony, "Honey, this is Arkansas. We don't have unions here."

My first negotiation and here's how it went. He offered $25 an appearance; I asked for $50. A very short time later we settled on $37.50 and, for $37.50 an appearance, my television career was launched at KATV News in Little Rock, Arkansas, twice a week.

A guppy can feel like a big fish in a small pond, and this particular guppy, dressed in what passed for fashion in Arkansas in the mid-1980s—big hair, long skirts, monster shoulder pads, still overweight, and let's not even mention the make-up—was no different. In time, I became a bigger fish, and people around began to recognize me—my first, if tiny, taste of fame. Even so, I felt I needed to know more to do it right. In medicine, doctors read journals and literature, go to meetings and conferences to learn new things which they then can incorporate into their practices. Where do you go, I asked, to learn television? The answer was: nowhere. Learn on the job.

I really didn't believe it, and thought I knew better. I'd heard about a meeting in Salt Lake City of the Radio-Television News Directors Association (RTNDA) and figured maybe there was something I could learn there. I packed up my infant daughter, Kate, and went to every course and lecture, and actually learned some things. It was the heyday of big spending in television—at the parties, the premium liquor flowed and huge lobsters and other flown-in goodies were the standard fare—and I did as much networking as a person can when she has a drooling, cooing baby in her arms.

But the most important connection was made by literally putting myself in the right place at the right time. Waiting in my hotel lobby, I struck up a conversation with a man who turned out to be an agent. In answer to his friendly questions—Kate gurgling the whole time—I rattled off what I'd done on air and why I found myself in Salt Lake, and he asked if I would send him a tape of my work.

I went home, mailed off the tape, and promptly forgot about it. Two weeks later he called to say he hoped I didn't mind but he'd sent the tape to *Good Morning America*. They liked it and wanted to fly me to New York to tape a few segments with Joan Lunden.

Wow.

Off I went. It'd been years since I'd been to New York City and I had never been there alone, but I felt really good. I was picked up at the airport and taken to a hotel where *Good Morning America* had a block of rooms. Because I was just a prospect, the producers decided not to have me on as a live guest—avoiding the possibility of a few moments of lethally dull live television—but instead, had Joan tape two segments with me after the broadcast. Joan was very gracious and I was, to put it kindly, uneven. One appearance—the better of the two—a show-and-tell with an empty soda bottle and cotton which demonstrated exactly how much tar and nicotine a single cigarette deposited in the lungs, made air. Thankfully, no one—myself included—even remembers what the second segment was. But the people at ABC saw the diamond in the rough, and in 1987 they hired me to do medical reports at scale for *Good Morning America*. This time, I got more than $37.50.

And I was on my way.

∞

If my television career started with a bit of luck, keeping it going had much more to do with commitment than anything else. When *Good Morning America* gave me a shot, I worked hard to get as good at it as I could. I learned how to judge time and read the teleprompter without either looking dull and stiff or tripping over my own words. (The teleprompter is supposed to be easy, but I actually had to practice reading slowly and carefully to sound natural.) I learned to be comfortable using my own ability to talk off the cuff and even let myself laugh every now and then. I took it in stride—well, okay, I heard her loud and clear—when a woman instrumental in hiring me at *Good Morning America* reminded me that the clothes that were fine for Little Rock (I first appeared on air in a black-and-white polka dot dress with three-quarter sleeves and huge shoulder pads) weren't quite what was needed for national television. I even learned how to sit still for the makeup sessions that make me look as good as I can, although I've never quite managed to lose the ten pounds it was suggested I get rid of at the very beginning. I'm happy to report that my hair passed muster from the start, but I never did get into wearing the high heels that were supposed to make my legs look longer.

I have even managed to learn to watch myself on television and get used to the bad stumble, the missed opportunity, the bad hair day, and the camera angle that gives me sixteen chins, or focuses, inopportunely, below my waist. Invariably, I wish I'd done it just a bit differently, but that, too, is part of the learning curve.

Television, like anything else, takes work, and I took learning my craft as seriously as I had the study of medicine. The shows on which I regularly appear— *Good Morning America* and *20/20*—require slightly different skills. On *GMA*, which is live television, I usually have three minutes to get a story out and shaped, and every second counts. If I waste the first forty-five seconds—if I can't quite find the right word, if I'm not 100-percent focused—it's not likely to be a wonderful or particularly useful three minutes of television. When I've worked as a co-host, I've learned that being really good—and I mean really good—at what you do for two hours straight (minus the news breaks and commercials) is a very high bar, and it doesn't often happen.

For 20/20, on the other hand, a twelve minute story takes days of shooting and, since it's taped, there is much more control over both how the correspondent looks and sounds and the cohesion of the story. This show is a bit different: My role is that of interviewer, and my job is to elicit the most cogent and illuminating answers from the people I'm interviewing. At the end, I try to pull the pieces together for the viewer. Experience builds on experience and, over the years, I've gotten more confident and better at what I do. I've also learned to listen to the criticisms and advice of the other professionals I work with, and that, too, has helped.

And, when all else fails, I remind myself that no one will ever see me in reruns . . .

In television, I learned I couldn't wait for opportunities to find me. I bullied and badgered (nicely, but indefatigably) to be a fill-in co-host and, finally, wore my boss down in 1991. He gave me a try, and I've been doing it ever since.

Television has given me a bigger vision of the world than I ever expected to have. Whenever I can, I've tried to be able to report outside the medical field with which I'm primarily associated and that has made my work in television an important and sustaining place of intellectual and experiential growth in my life.

I've interviewed ordinary people who have had extraordinary things happen to them. I've interviewed Nobel laureates and Somali warlords, and some of the movers and shakers who have left their mark on our world. Each experience has taught me something. What other line of work would have me cooking *coq au vin* with Julia Child in Burgundy? (We had to convince her that, despite its authenticity, using the chicken's blood as part of the sauce wasn't something America was ready for, not first thing in the morning!) How else would I have found myself in Saudi Arabia, in the midst of Operation Desert Shield, or, more recently, at refugee camps near Kosovo? There, I met doctors, bankers, computer experts, college professors, and musicians. They were my peers but their circumstances, through accidents of history and geography, could not have been more different, and I was sobered by how quickly and terribly the normal order of things can change. There, too, I met a thirteen-year-old girl, the same age as my daughter Kate, who found herself literally alone in the world—separated from her parents, in a tent with nine strangers—and I wept for her and all the other lost children. I returned to America with my eyes adjusted to the importance of ordinary things, and held my children just a bit more tightly than usual.

I have become a person of richer fabric because of this other career I never planned on but which became a major part of my life. I consider myself particularly lucky to be involved in two fields that keep me constantly stimulated and learning. Being a physician grounds me and keeps whatever fame being on television bestows in perspective; none of that matters when I am in the operating room and my patient is hemorrhaging or I am at the bedside of someone who is terminally ill. At the same time, the visibility television offers has permitted me to speak out on important issues pertaining to women and health, while the financial compensation permits me to see any patient—regardless of his or her ability to pay—so that I can practice medicine in the truest sense.

I am equally grateful for every opportunity that's come my way and, in the midst of a sometimes tumultuous life, for having the good sense to take advantage of them. I guess what I'm saying is this: My television career may have started by accident, but that it continued was no accident at all.

And I, for one, keep looking at the horizon, to see what's next.

∞

Women can re-imagine themselves anytime they choose to; there's no right or wrong time and no time that's ever too late. If we take the time to look around us, we will find plenty of inspiration in our own communities as well as in public life, in volunteerism and in paying work. My mother went back to school at the age of sixty-nine and, fueled by a lifelong love for tending the earth, took a master gardening class. She nows works as a volunteer, restoring gardens and public spaces in my hometown of Fort Wayne. She is also part of a program that, in conjunction with the local agricultural extension, educates inner-city children about plants and gardening, and puts them in contact—usually their only contact—with a garden and, ultimately, the cycles of the earth and nature. My friend Connie, a gifted and successful clothing designer, found a new passion in her commitment, fifteen or so years ago, to the plight of children in need of adoptive parents all over the globe. She has traveled the world, bringing children to the United States to new parents who embraced them. Her own life has a fullness because of the gifts she brings to others' lives and the gifts her own two adopted children have, in turn, given back to her and her husband. Her creativity—so evident in the way she drapes fabric or cuts a sleeve—simply found another outlet.

We can take heart from the examples prominent women offer. Lady Bird Johnson, widow of a president, devoted herself to raising America's consciousness about the country's natural resources, its legacies of beauty and wildflowers, and succeeded to inspire people and programs alike. Actress Elizabeth Taylor has used her celebrity to draw attention to causes such as AIDS, helping to give a terrifying disease a human face.

We can seek inspiration from the tireless Julia Child who, after a career in the OSS that took her to India, China, and other far-flung parts of the world, attended her first cooking class at the age of thirty-seven at Paris's Cordon Bleu, and published her first cookbook, *Mastering the Art of French Cooking*, at age forty-nine, after working on it for ten years. At fifty, she starred in educational television's first cooking program, with Julia, in her own words, "careening around the stove" in grainy black-and-white, and inspiring women to take their cooking seriously, in what was traditionally a man's field. By the time *The French Chef* finally burst into living color, she was two years shy of sixty. For someone who started "late," she is still, now in her late eighties, going strong, mentoring new chefs, male and female alike.

And then there's the amazing, improbable, and magical story of Anna Mary Robertson Moses, better known as "Grandma Moses," whose work gave America a new understanding of simple beauty. She was born in 1860, at a time when girls only went to school three summer months of the year (it was thought too cold in the winter, particularly with inadequate clothing). At the age of twelve, she became a "hired girl" for an elderly couple—cleaning, tending, cooking—until her marriage at the age of twenty-seven, when the work she'd previously done for others sustained her own family instead. She bore ten children and buried five, and, as a farmer's wife, she lived busy chore-filled days. Widowed at the age of sixty-seven, she didn't take up art until her late seventies—first, stitching pictures in worsted wool and then, painting—and only then because housekeeping had become too strenuous for her.

And so, for the next quarter of a century until her death at 101, Grandma Moses painted scenes of a simpler past already lost to modern America and, in doing so, helped people think a bit differently about the journey of life.

∽∞∾

We need to encourage each other as adventurers and remind each other and ourselves that the path that's right for one part of our lives may not be the right path for the next. When we talk to our daughters, we need to remember that the question isn't "What do you want to be when you grow up?" but "Who do you want to be?" We need to remind them that the "who" we are changes over time, is grown and given shape by different life experiences, and that there is always time to change your mind and choose a different, more satisfying path.

I am often asked when I will give up medicine to concentrate on television full-time. It occurs to me that, usually, the question is asked by a man, and I think I understand why. The traditional male model of succcess values an early sense of direction and focus on a single goal. The decision of "what" to be is usually made in a man's twenties, implemented in his thirties and early and mid-forties.

But here's the question I ask: Why should I have to choose between my careers, when each gives me something of value? Perhaps—only perhaps—I could have made more money concentrating on just one, except that wasn't all I was looking for. Maybe, just maybe, I need a model of my own.

We need to recognize that women will never be totally comfortable with the choices they make until they find a model of success that suits each woman personally. For one thing, there is the cyclical nature of our bodies and the simple truth that the finite period of time in which we can choose to bear and raise children coincides with the years that, in the male model of success, are devoted to establishing and solidifying career. The extraordinary growth of female entrepreneurship—according to a 1998 study conducted by Catalyst and the National Association of Women Business Owners, one in four U.S. company workers is employed by a woman-owned business—shows that women are actively seeking solutions to fulfilling their multifaceted and changing goals in life. The study also revealed the adventuresome spirit that sets women apart; 56 percent of the businesses started by women are unrelated to their previous careers. Of those businesses, 14 percent seek to turn a personal avocation into a money-making proposition. (In contrast, only 36 percent of male entrepreneurs try something new. Fifty-nine percent stick to what they know.)

We need to cheer on every new and creative solution to the choices posed by a woman's journey.

Maybe, too, when we admit that the nature of our bodies is a real component of who each of us is, then we'll also be able to recognize that what in the male model may be considered "circuituous" may be, for the female of the species, the path that lets us be more than one self at a time, an echo of the journey the moon takes in the night sky and in our bodies.

So be it.

Wake-Up Calls

❦

SOMETIMES, THE JOURNEY takes us into the unexpected, into junctures where we lose our bearings and equilibrium and where the easy flow of day-to-day life is painfully interrupted. These places—where we confront sickness, tragedy, and mortality—test our souls and change us in myriad ways. These are the intersections that challenge our faith as well as our vision of the workings of the world and sometimes push us to live our lives with greater meaning and commitment.

Up until the first months of 1986, I'd been a skater on life's surfaces. My days filled, there was little time to ponder the direction my life was taking or the choices I was making. It was an unexamined life in every sense of the word.

Sometimes, though, an unseen hand forces us to take stock. Sometimes, we need to gain a sense of the ending that comes to all living things to live life with greater meaning.

Even then, we do not grow all at once but by fits and starts. I know now that what happened in those months was a preparation for the first of the truly important choices I would make in my life.

⌘

I was diagnosed with cancer on my thirty-fourth birthday. Just a few days before, my voice had begun to sound raspy and my throat felt sore. I'd felt tired for a few weeks but my work-filled schedule in those days before I had children, when I was a surgeon at the University of Arkansas, was grueling and so I thought nothing of it. Then, getting into scrubs for surgery one morning, I tucked my hair up into a cap and saw an egg-sized lump in my neck. Chills and fever soon followed. My skin became dotted with tiny hemorrhages. as the level of platelets that help clot the blood fell precipitiously.

My life screeched to a halt and, in a totally unexpected turn of events, the doctor became a patient.

I turned to Laura, a colleague and a female oncologist my own age, to handle my case. The most hopeful diagnoses—mononucleosis or Hodgkin's disease—were quickly ruled out, and I found myself hearing what no one ever wants to: that I had a rare type of lymph node cancer, which very few people survive. It was rare enough, in fact, that only experimental—not standard— courses of treatment were recommended. Forcing myself to hear my doctor's words was hard, but absorbing the look in her eyes harder still.

First-hand, I experienced the dislocation of the patient thought to be gravely ill. Over the next few days, the drumbeat of the hospital—the comings and goings of hospital personnel, the scheduling of batteries of tests, the punctual delivery of pills and food—was the only rhythm of my life. I felt the way Jonah must have, swallowed whole inside the whale.

Batteries of tests filled the hours of my day. A needle biopsy. An excision of the lump. An MRI, which nearly ended in disaster when I had an anaphylactic reaction to the dye. A bone-marrow biopsy. I was alternately terrified and grief-stricken, angry and determined.

As I waited for my doctor to perform the bone-marrow biopsy, lying on the cold, steel table, a white sheet draped over me, I started talking to myself, fast and furious. In my head, at least, the words became shouts: "I am not ready to die. I haven't done enough, lived enough, accomplished enough. This isn't fair."

The monologue came to an abrupt halt with the sting of the local anesthetic that was to numb the surrounding tissue. Never, ever, I vowed to myself, would I minimize the pain of a procedure to a patient if I survived this. The pain of the bone-marrow biopsy was awesome and soul-shattering; had I been standing, it would have brought me to my knees. I have never forgotten it, a level of pain that the hard labor of childbirth doesn't even approach.

I was an obedient patient, distinguished only by one small act of rebellion. With a low white blood cell count and the experimental treatment still ahead of me, my doctors worried about the risk of infection. They wanted to keep in me in the hospital, in isolation. Instead I insisted that I be able to go home, to the house I shared with my second husband.

And then, just as abruptly as life in the hospital had swallowed me up, I was spit back out into the world to await the results of the tests and the opinions of three highly respected experts on lymphoma in two days' time.

I remember walking out into the cool, crisp sunlight of an early spring day in Little Rock, the trees just in bud, surrounded by sounds and movement: car engines starting, the low rumble of buses, the stray bits of conversation overheard on crowded streets. I remember feeling both angry and astonished that life could go on in such a perfectly ordinary way, as if this were just any Friday in March, without any regard to what was happening to me.

All the activities by which I defined myself—the surgery, the rounds, the patient examinations, the grant applications, even the community lectures—were easily, too easily, assigned to other doctors. Whatever idea I had of my own indispensability was rudely, painfully adjusted. The surface of my life stripped away, I found I had little to hold on to, save the love of family and friends.

I retreated to the living room couch and the hammock slung between the pine trees in the backyard. I could have no company—my doctors thought the risk of infection too high with my severely compromised immune system—so the telephone was my only connection to the outside world. Bundled up against the chill of the early spring, I lay in the hammock, watching the flow of the sunlight through the trees, seeing different tints in the landscape lit in turn as if by the slow glow of a candle. As I rocked back and forth, my mind wandered from memories of my childhood to the small things in my life left undone, like the unwashed laundry piled on my bedroom floor. I felt somehow suspended in time, cut loose from the quotidian.

Why was I meant to die? No matter how hard I tried, I seemed incapable of understanding, of processing, what I knew as a physician: that, if the diagnosis was true, there was little hope.

But severed from the ordinary in those few days, I was forced to look below the surface for connection. In a reversal of lifelong roles, I tried to comfort my distraught parents, playing the optimistic cheerleader to deflect their pain. I no longer saw them as just my parents and guardians but as vulnerable and worried, struggling, as every human being does, for answers in the face of what seemed a violation of nature: the possible death of a child. I saw that they coped no better than I when confronted with the fragile nature of human existence and the bonds that give life meaning. In seeing them as human, I loved them even more.

Lying in the hammock, realizing what was at stake, the world around me came forth with amazing clarity, as if all of my senses had been sharpened. The feel of my dog Jenna's head under my outstretched hand, the sight of Freeway the cat asleep in a narrow shaft of sunlight, the sweet morning scent of pine needles on damp earth. I awakened to detail and, even now, all these years later, I recognize that what I gained that weekend still stays with me, no matter where I am.

It was also the longest weekend of my life.

Monday morning, I took a deep breath and went back to the hospital, fully expecting the worse. Instead, there were new questions. The experts had weighed in, and two out of three ventured that it wasn't cancer but a virus masquerading as one. The third doctor was unsure, and recommended another bone marrow biopsy, a fate I wasn't eager to be consigned to.

A new team of doctors was called in, this time infectious disease specialists. I stood stripped in an examination room, my nipples puckered and my bare feet cold on the tiles, while they pored over every inch of my body, poking and prodding. Standing there that day, I learned something about myself and about medicine. My literal physical exposure, my nakedness, was nothing compared to my emotional exposure, my desperate dependence on them to come up with answers and help. I don't know what I looked like to them—my eyes hollow and desperate—but I know what I felt: I relied on the human beings in white coats who surrounded me that day as I'd never relied on anyone before or since.

One of the doctors looked up. There were some

enlarged lymph nodes in my right groin. Had they always been there? "No," I answered. "I noticed them after being bitten by a tick." I rode horses in those days, as I do now, and the scrubby woods around Little Rock were filled with ticks.

And with that seemingly inconsequential exchange—I even wondered why he'd asked—they finally had something to work with. Amazingly, what had begun as a problem beyond medical reach was swiftly understood as something easily, eminently fixable. I was rightly diagnosed with tularemia—rabbit-skinner's disease—a tick-borne illness—curable with nothing more complicated than a course of antibiotics and a month of bed rest.

Even though in time I recovered completely, I would, in some sense, never go back to precisely where I'd been or who I'd been before. My firsthand experience as a patient—the terrible wait of the weekend, the stripping away of self that takes place lying alone in a hospital bed, the desperate dependence on the intelligence and training of strangers—made me a better, more compassionate doctor, sensitive to my own patients' fears and anxieties as they waited for news. I saw, for the first time, that news—even bad news—is a patient's emotional lifeline, always to be preferred to the limbo of not knowing. I would never again feel that choosing the "right time" to tell a patient of his or her status was up to me.

My first real understanding of what it means to be born mortal began, slowly, to inform my spirit.

But I was lucky that time, fourteen years ago, in a way that thousands of women each year are not, to have a terrible diagnosis so quickly and simply reversed. I experienced seventy-two hours of hell but, when they were over, they were done with, and to those of you reading these words, who've not had the benefit of speedy reprieve, as I might not the next time, I hope you're with me on this: These dark places have much to teach us all. They are places where gifts are hidden, for us and those around us, if we only look. Even squinting at endings lets us each envision new beginnings and lets us begin to pay attention to what matters to us.

The required month of bed rest—which, of course, I fought—shifted my vision in subtle ways. Lying in the hammock or on the living room couch, alone and exiled from the activities that had always filled and given meaning to my days, I finally was forced to think about myself and where I was in life. Introspection doesn't come easily to me, but it felt as though so much had happened in such a very short time that I had no choice but to think.

The extraordinary vulnerability I'd felt in the hospital couldn't just be banished out of hand and, in the quiet among the pine trees, I had to concede that there was much in life beyond my or anyone else's control. For the first time, rather than deny the part of life that wasn't in my hands or anyone else's, I realized that, in order to go forward, I had to take control of what I could. I have never lived the same way since: I listen to my body when it's tired, and consider the balance of rest and activity absolutely vital to living every day.

Since that time, each year on my birthday, as a way of honoring and respecting myself, I schedule the necessary battery of tests—a physical, a pelvic exam, a mammogram, a colonoscopy—so that I know I have controlled the aspects of my life that I can.

I heard this part of the wake-up call loud and clear. And it is the only sermon I know that is worth preaching from every rooftop: Respect yourself and your body, and take what responsibility you can for it. Once a year at least, put yourself resolutely and firmly first. Remind yourself, your sisters, your mother, your girlfriends, your neighbors.

There were other things, too, that began, bit by bit, as a result of what happened that March, to find a place in my field of vision. I began to realize what merely living on the surface might, in the end, mean to me or, better put, keep me from experiencing. Like most perceptions, this came gradually and, while the first seeds of my spiritual awakening were sown that spring, they would take years to harvest.

As it happens, I had much, much more to learn.

∞

Just a month or so after I'd gone back to work and life had taken on its old, familiar rhythms, the phone rang, very late at night.

I was frightened the minute I heard my father's voice. He had had his yearly physical and, since his own father had died of cancer of the colon, he had persuaded his doctor to give him a colonoscopy instead of a proctoscopy, since it reveals more of the bowel's area. He was, somehow, uneasy about his health and thought he should be checked out as thoroughly as possible.

The test revealed a mass, embedded in the bowel wall. It required surgery. The biopsy confirmed the mass was abnormal.

There was, in his case, no hope of a misdiagnosis, and his surgery was to take place the day after tomorrow. And, no, he didn't need any of his children to come home to Fort Wayne.

We disobeyed his wishes en masse and, upon arrival, I found myself in the midst of an impromptu family gathering that was distinguished mainly by unani-mous, full-scale denial and the slightly raucous humor of a close-knit family. Despite the fact that all of us were adults, technically at least, and two of us—my brother and I—were doctors who well understood what our father was up against, the idea that something bad could actually happen to either of our parents was unthinkable and impossible to absorb.

Many of us remain children long after we leave our childhood homes, and I, at least, was no different.

Amazingly enough, my father became the model patient, determined—as he always is—to beat the situa-tion. The family pulled together—the two medical types on one side, the two who hate hospitals as close to the door as possible—with my mother occupying the middle ground, on the side of the bed away from the catheters and drains. His indomitable spirit aided his recovery and, five days later, he was ready to go home. The morn-ing my father was to be discharged, my brother did what I was simply thinking about doing—he grabbed Dad's charts from the nurse's station—and came upon the pathologist's report which had not yet been shared with the patient or his family. I read over his shoulder and the looks on our faces betrayed us instantly to our physician father. He demanded that it be read aloud.

The report was not as unambiguous as we might

have hoped. Several of the lymph nodes adjacent to the bowel walls were cancerous; most narrowly interpreted, this meant that the tumor had metastasized. Seen more optimistically, though, it told us that only two of the nodes were affected, while the others were clear. Statistically, the report meant this: My father's rate of cure had dropped to roughly 30 percent. In any group of three patients, two are likely to die, and my father, typically, responded that he felt sorry for the other two unlucky bastards.

But black humor aside, in 1986 there were few options open to him. Chemotherapy did not increase survival rates for colon cancer and, moreover, would take a terrible, literally sickening, toll on his body. Radiation therapy would cause scarring and set him up for future bowel obstructions. Doing nothing, though, left open the possibility that errant cancer cells would set up shop elsewhere in his body.

My father took his destiny in hand, and took the chance. And he, a conventionally trained surgeon, started using visual imagery—without knowing anything about what is now known as pyschoneuroimmunology —willing the tumor to be cured and the cancer cells to die. He imagined his own will as a giant predator, gobbling up the cancerous cells in its wake. And he re-embraced life, opening up his imagination, paying attention to the details around him, and as he's told me, the nuances and shades and colors of everything that surrounds him changed forever. The changes in him took place at the very core of his being.

And, as I write this, he has been cancer-free for nearly fourteen years.

∽◈∼

Wake-up calls are just a beginning; whatever spiritual or personal evolution comes out of these hard parts of the journey is largely up to the individual. Nothing of importance can be learned easily or automatically, and we owe it to ourselves, at these moments of crisis, to glean whatever opportunities they offer us.

My family's near brushes with death during those crowded months in 1986 altered how I saw life and its rhythms, but the important truths were, then, just glimpsed, not wholly owned. I'd like to be able to say that these events together formed a true epiphany letting me see the essence of life clearly and fully, but it didn't happen that way. I don't think, except perhaps in fiction and in the rarest of instances, that people so easily grasp what gives life meaning nor, for that matter, do they see what they need to do for themselves to live happier, more fulfilled lives.

The journey does not give up its truths so easily.

Experiencing the fragility of life directly, confrontationally, changed what I knew and how I knew it. My intellectual knowledge of death was given a real, personal, and emotional context, and I began to understand truly the way in which life is indeed a gift. There is a wonderful teaching story, a parable in the Zen tradition that is attributed to Buddha, and it says what I learned simply and evocatively and better than I can:

> A man traveling across a field encountered a tiger. He fled, the tiger after him. Coming to a precipice, he caught hold of the root of a wild vine and swung himself down over the edge. The tiger sniffed at him from above. Trembling, the man looked down to where, far below, another tiger was waiting to eat him. Only the vine sustained him.
>
> Two mice, one white and one black, little by little started to gnaw away the vine. The man saw a luscious strawberry near him. Grasping the vine with one hand, he plucked the strawberry with the other. How sweet it tasted!

How else—except when we are faced with the fragility of the vine, our literal lifeline—can we taste life's sweetness? I can only say that I became a thankful person in the truest sense when, each year, my father's tests came back clean and clear.

Because of my own experience, I became a wiser, kinder doctor and woman. Because of my father's, I began to understand the true connection between body and spirit.

But the other ways in which I changed were much more subtle. For the first time, I began to look below life's surface, and to pay attention to the things that were important to me. I began, in small ways, to acknowledge the needs of an inner self that wasn't fed just by my outer accomplishments—my work in the hospital, in the community, and on television—but which needed other, deeper connections.

These were the first steps I took toward listening to my heart.

⌒∞⌒

Every year, thousands of women will receive wake-up calls of their own. There are few among us who cannot name a relative or friend who has had to confront her own mortality. According to the American Cancer Society, among the diseases a woman is most likely to confront, in order of the occurrence in the population, is cancer; 598,000 new cases will be diagnosed. This year, 175,000 cases of breast cancer will be diagnosed, 77,600 cases of lung cancer, 51,000 cases of colon cancer, and 26,200 cases of ovarian cancer. Heart disease which, though still commonly perceived as a "man's disease," is, in fact, the leading cause of death among women, responsible for one out of every two deaths.

Taking care of ourselves—making time to be our own caretakers—is the first step. Moderation is the key word. Watch what you eat but don't deny yourself occasional goodies. Don't smoke. And exercise. If every woman did these things, one-half of the heart disease and almost one-third of the cancers in this country could be prevented. Having ourselves checked is the second step we must all take. Pick a special date—it can be your birthday, an anniversary, or any date you choose—and consider it carved in stone. Become a participant in deciding the kinds of tests that need to be scheduled. If you have a family history of disease—heart disease or cancer—be proactive. Sit down and make a list of the diseases or conditions for which you may be at risk. Talk to your doctor about what tests should be tailored to your needs and at what age you should start getting them. Because of my father's diagnosis of colon cancer and my grandfather's death from the disease, I have had, since turning forty, a yearly colonoscopy, as have my siblings. Follow your instincts. As a physician, I know that the majority of illnesses are first detected—or better put, felt or intuited—by the patient herself. Even if you are not normally assertive, insist that your doctor listen to your concerns and test you accordingly. Remember: It's your body and your life.

The third crucial step is to be an informed patient. Should you get a diagnosis that requires medical intervention, take the time to inform yourself about the disease, and feel free to ask your doctors as many questions as you want. If you are dissatisfied with his or her responses, seek another opinion. It is your life, after all. Finally, don't feel as though you need to go it alone. We can listen to what the wake-up call has to teach us if we are in the company of those who can help us through the dark passages. All over America, there are circles of women who can help you find the way.

And finally, we all need to remember that there is opportunity in every crisis. It heartens my soul to remind myself that the two—"crisis" and "opportunity"—are so closely linked that, in at least one language on the planet, Chinese, there is a single word for both.

Listening to the Heart

SOMETIMES, LIFE'S intersections are filled with magic so powerful that every detail stays vivid in the mind through the passage of time, illuminated and thrown into high relief as if lit by a huge, shimmering full moon on a dark, cloudless summer night. These moments are rare but when they happen—if they happen—they fill our souls with a special kind of brightness, and we feel as though we are looking into the very core of everything that matters in life. At these moments, we know what we know with sureness and with amazing clarity.

True epiphanies are rare, but they do happen.

The journey has taught me to listen to my heart. I look at the false starts and detours in my life—marriages, jobs, relationships—and I can see what they have in common. More than once, I was fulfilling other people's expectations, doing what looked right to the world, not what felt right to me. I didn't know then what I know now: What the world thinks of me is none of my business.

What prevented me from listening to my heart was simple: I hadn't yet learned to trust it. I got lucky, though. One night, I was offered a choice so pure, so big, so important that no amount of rationalization could even begin to get in the way.

I think someone was watching over me to make sure that, this time, I got it right.

∞

On July 26, 1986, the telephone rang. It was a Saturday night in Little Rock, Arkansas, where I lived, and I was getting dressed to go out to a party with my second husband. The caller identified himself as a family doctor from Fort Smith, Arkansas, and while I didn't recognize his name, he said he remembered me from when he'd been a medical student on the ear, nose, and throat service. I had, he thought, been very nice to him. I still couldn't quite place him. He'd heard, through the medical grapevine, that I had had a miscarriage, and he asked both about my health and whether my husband and I had a child yet.

I replied that I was fine and that, no, we didn't have a child.

It turned out he was calling because the private adoption he had arranged for a bright fifteen-year-old, a patient he'd seen through prenatal care, had suddenly fallen through. The young girl, the birth father, and her parents had decided to give the baby up but the prospective adoptive family had suddenly gotten cold feet and, with only weeks to go in the pregnancy, the doctor had no alternatives. Did we want to adopt the child?

I made up my mind in an instant. My heart, not my brain, said "yes." I don't remember exactly what I replied but I managed to tell him I'd call him back. My then husband, hearing my news, was—to put it mildly—less than enthusiastic, and it didn't take very long for the discussion to become a fight. His was the voice of reason. He pointed out how self-indulgent our life was. We were living well and liking it. We had no time for a baby now. My ambitions and my career. His work. Our life. We needed to wait. The next time would be the right time. His argument was rational. I don't remember his words exactly but that's probably just as well.

I knew there would be no next time. I found

myself at an intersection with a meaning and a purpose, and recognized instantly that if there was a cosmic pattern, this was it. Maybe I knew because I had been a pediatrician, and understood the amazing, implausible cosmic magic of conception, how two simple cells could unite and evolve into a multibillion-cellular being unlike any other on the planet. Maybe it was all the stories I knew of couples struggling to conceive or waiting years to adopt. Or maybe, in and around the echoes of the doctor's question, I suddenly knew something else: An important part of my life was empty.

For most women, motherhood is an obvious, conscious choice, but it hadn't been for me. During medical school I'd seriously considered not having children. For one thing, I had had the best mother in the world, and I knew I could never measure up to her example. She was a stay-at-home mom who gave up a budding career in art to be with four children, and she was and is amazingly good at the fine art and hard work of motherhood. She juggled three scout troops at once, designed and sewed costumes, made enough bake sale cookies to feed a small country, cheered us on, and checked thousands of pages of homework. She was fun, loving, and always there for us. How could I possibly do all that and be a doctor too?

I didn't have enough faith in myself to believe that I could be a good mother in another, if different, way. My blinders firmly strapped on, I just focused on being the best surgeon I could be, and left that other part of my life unexamined.

But the phone call changed all that. At the age of thirty-four, the neglected corners of my inner landscape were suddenly brightly lit. And I knew with complete certainty that my destiny was somehow linked to this still unborn life. This was no accident; I knew at the core of my being that this was meant to be.

My husband and I were at loggerheads all Saturday night and well into Sunday. It's clear now, though it wasn't then, that the differences between us were meaningful and profound. We resolved nothing that weekend but, when Monday came, I reassured myself that we had a few weeks to sort things out. I would somehow manage to bring him around before the baby was born. Monday morning I was out shooting a story for channel 7, KATV, the ABC affiliate in Little Rock, when the doctor called again. The birth mother had gone into labor two weeks early, and there was a healthy, seven-pound, two-ounce baby girl in the hospital. Did we want her?

Nothing on this earth could have stopped me from going to Fort Smith. I called my husband and gave him the news in a conversation that probably wouldn't ever qualify as "dialogue." I like to think I won him over but, in retrospect, he probably just gave up trying to change my mind. I took a look at the house in which two child-less working people lived, and I knew I needed to shop. I drove a Suburban in those days and backed the truck up to the door of a children's store. I walked in, told the lady I was adopting a baby, and needed "stuff." She asked me if I had receiving blankets and when I asked her what a receiving blanket was, she knew I was in trouble and that she had a job to do. Hard to believe but, even as a former pediatrician, I was clueless! I drove off fully equipped with all the paraphernalia a new mother and a baby need, and then some. I called my partners in the medical practice and told them about the new change in my life; they surprised me by turning an empty office in the suite into a nursery so that I wouldn't lose any time at work.

My younger sister, Martha, who'd moved to Little Rock with me, helped me get the baby's room together in what had to be a world's record of some sort. Taking care of all the details only heightened the anticipation and, by Tuesday afternoon, when my husband, my sister, and I piled into the car to drive to Fort Smith, all of us—even my husband—were excited and happy.

Arkansas is hot in the summer, and this sunny July day was no exception; the car thermometer registered a blistering 107 degrees at three in the afternoon when we pulled out of the driveway. Fort Smith is 160 miles northwest of Little Rock, almost on the Oklahoma border, and the drive takes about three hours. My husband drove, and from the passenger seat window, I watched the landscape change from rolling hills punctuated by flat fields of feed corn, framed by distant Arkansas pines, to the foothills of the Ozark Mountains. I remember feeling as though something in me was opening up, blossoming, as each passing mile brought me closer to my daughter. I'm always surprised when women talk about bonding with their babies during pregnancy and breastfeeding as if these were the only times or ways that bonding takes place. For me, the process started with that Saturday night phone call.

I was already on the way to becoming this baby girl's mother. I had given her a name and, now, all I needed to do was hold her in my arms.

We arrived at the small community hospital where we were directed to the nursery. You know what the nursery looks like: There's always a big glass window, and through this one, we could see neat rows of plastic bassinets, eighteen of them, each with a baby inside.

To my sister's amazement, I pointed her out. There was Kate, my dark-haired, round-faced daughter. I had wanted her first name to sound strong, to be a name that let people know she could take care of herself, and it has turned out to be a name that fits her fine. The nurse put her in my arms, a tiny bundle wrapped in a pale pink receiving blanket, a little hat perched on her head. The entire way home, the new mother in me marveled at her perfection and my incredible good fortune, while my doctor side checked to make sure every hole was in place, every finger and toe accounted for. Never one to leave anything medical to chance—even though, yes, I had read the hospital pediatrican's report—I checked and rechecked, even listening to her heart and lungs with my ear pressed to her chest.

For all that I felt that day—the amazing connection to the child in my arms, as if the two of us were interlocking pieces of a puzzle—I had no inkling of the incredible magic Kate would bring into my life as she continues to and always will.

On the drive back to Little Rock, with Kate safely strapped into the car seat by my side in the back, the day gave way to early evening, softening the landscape beyond the interstate. Later, the rays of the setting sun seemed to shine in only on the two of us before evening became night. Still later, walking up the driveway with her in my arms, the pretty little gabled brick house in which we lived became a different kind of home.

಄

Looking back at that particular intersection of my life fills me with wonder and gratitude. Part of the wonder is Kate herself. Sensitive, talented, and artistic, she has, from the moment I first held her in my arms, made my world a different and a better place. She has nourished my soul and, now, as she stands on the threshold of her own womanhood, I can only hope that I have nourished hers in more than equal measure. Then, too, there is the wonder of how Kate became my daughter. I have come to believe that she was chosen to be a part of my path in this lifetime. The phone call that night wasn't a lucky accident or a coincidence but something else entirely, rare and beautiful. It was one of a handful of moments in my life so far that have offered me a vision of the workings of a universe filled with spirit, purpose, and meaning, the closest I think I will ever get to glimpsing the hand of God.

I am grateful not just for the gift of Kate but for that moment of real insight that let me know and choose with stubborn, unyielding clarity. I am thankful that I could not be dissuaded by argument or anger or even my own fear of failing as a mother, and that I had the guts and the determination to listen to my own inner voice. Although I didn't know it at the time, the marriage I was in would run its course in just a few years' time. It would founder for other reasons but, with the benefit of hindsight, I can see that where we each stood that Saturday night in Little Rock spoke volumes about what we were and weren't to each other. Past that intersection, the road ahead as the single mother of two girls was hard and sometimes lonely, but it was the road that brought me to where I am and who I am today.

Late at night when I'm up alone and the house is quiet, I check on each of my three children in turn, as I suppose sleepless women everywhere do. I love all my children wholly and completely but, sometimes, in Kate's room, hearing the slow, even breathing of a well-loved child fast asleep, I get back in touch with the sheer wonder of it—the miracle or magic that brought Kate into my life—and I'm flooded with feeling. It is sobering to realize that had I hesitated that night, if I hadn't chosen in a millisecond, two lives that were meant to be together would have missed each other. At that moment, I truly understood that a woman's ability to choose her own path—no matter how scary it sometimes feels—is perhaps the greatest of all gifts. I'm blessed that my oldest daughter is a constant and beautiful reminder that I must always listen to my own heart.

It's impossible now to imagine what my life would be like, let alone what I would be like, without my two daughters and my son. My work both as a doctor and a television correspondent has made me a different kind of mother than my mother was, but I've come to understand that "different" isn't a synonym for "better" or "worse." And while it's true that my bake sale cookies are likely to be store-bought as hers never were, I am there for my children in every important way that my mom was and continues to be there for me.

The choices I've made are very different from my mother's choices, just as, in time, my daughters' choices will be different from mine. As long as the choices my children make are the right ones for them, allowing them to set priorities that leave them feeling comfortable in their skins, it will not matter. I hope I inspire them, while encouraging them to find their own paths.

My choices are mine, and my life will never be a blueprint for anyone else to follow. That's true not only for me and my daughters but for every woman in America. Each of us needs to live a life that provides an example of how a woman's life can be lived with pleasure and satisfaction, without anyone insisting that it's the only example out there.

Listen to your heart. Trust your own voice.

A few years ago, while speaking to an audience of several hundred women, I was asked which was the most important part of my life: medicine, television, or motherhood. On the spot, I answered "motherhood" and was greeted by a round of applause. I felt myself beam with pride, but at the same time, I felt very uncomfortable.

On reflection, this isn't the question women need to ask each other or themselves. The real question is this: Does the work we do—whether that is the work of a stay-at-home mother or a job in the outside world—give each of us what we need?

When we are getting what we need—whether that's a feeling of accomplishment from supervising homework or performing surgery, an income that supports us or improves our lives, or a sense of independence—we feel strong, act strong, and get better at everything we do. Doing feeds the soul. What a woman does in her life isn't the point; it's how she feels about it. And how her work, whatever it is, fills her up and rounds her out.

I don't think it's possible to separate the different roles I play in my life—mother, wife, doctor, television correspondent—from one another. I have chosen each of those roles, listening to my own heart, and each contributes to the fabric of who I am. If the demands of medicine kept me from choosing motherhood at one point in my life, then equally the benefits of my career—my financial independence and the feeling of self-worth my work has always given me—made it possible for me to support and care for my children during those years when I was without a partner. Motherhood has made me a more compassionate and sensitive doctor but, then, the different kinds of work I do outside the home—from seeing patients to reporting on a story—keep me growing and learning as both a person and a parent.

Listen to your heart. Trust yourself. I know from experience how hard it is, but it is so necessary.

Someday soon, I want to take Kate by the hand, as I will take her sister in a few years' time and later her brother, for a walk on a summer's night, high upon a hill or mountain where we can see the roads below us crisscrossing the landscape. We will sit there together—with the intersections and roadways in plain view—and I will tell her my stories by the light of a shining moon.

And, with the world spread out before us, it will be Kate's turn—and then her siblings'—to talk, and mine to listen, as she plans for the roads ahead.

Going for Broke

⌒∞⌒

I HAD STARTED my life over, or so I
thought at the time, at the age of thirty-one. When I
moved to Little Rock to begin my medical career, I had
left the mistakes I'd made in Pittsburgh behind me, my
failed marriage chief among them, and begun anew. I
didn't understand then that when we refuse to let ourselves learn from the journeys we've taken, we simply
destine ourselves to walk the same path over and over,
no matter where we find ourselves geographically.

Starting over takes soul work. Starting over requires that we change the fundamental ways we see both ourselves and the choices we make.

I wasn't ready. I still didn't see the urgency of addressing the old issues of self-esteem and how I saw my self.

What happened in Little Rock would change all that. What amounted to a free fall down a mountain would, finally, begin to force me to look at my inner self.

Even so, the journey was circuituous.

∞

I ended up in Little Rock, Arkansas, not quite on purpose but not exactly by accident either. At the time, I thought accident had more to do with it than anything else but looking back, I don't think so. This was the part of my journey someone up there had deemed absolutely necessary, and the years in Little Rock were both some of the best and worst of my life.

It was the city in which I would finally be forced to try to come of age emotionally. It was where I became a mother for the first time. It was the place where, stripped of just about everything save my professional abilities and my daughter, I finally had to take stock of who I was. It was, in the end, the city I would have to leave to make myself whole.

My residency in Pittsburgh ended, and it was time, finally, to get my first job as a doctor. I had had my heart set on working in Chicago, at Northwestern University, where they needed a head and neck surgeon, and with my department chair's recommendation, it looked like a pretty sure thing. The interview arranged, I got on a plane, filled with confidence, and arrived in Chicago only to find out that the chairman of the department wasn't in. He had forgotten about the appointment. I ended up interviewing with junior staff members who couldn't hire me anyway, in the operating room during surgery, and that was that. I flew home empty handed: no job.

No opening at the University of Pittsburgh either. Finally, my department chair, Dr. Myers, suggested I call a colleague of his with whom he was writing a book, at the University of Arkansas for Medical Sciences. Arkansas? Me, in Arkansas? He kindly reminded me that I didn't have a job, no one was exactly beating down my door, and, well, basically who was I to be so cocky?

As it happens, professionally, the University of Arkansas was the best thing that could have happened to me.

I knew nothing really about Arkansas, or the city I was moving to. Flying in over the eastern part of the state, my nose pressed against the window, I saw acres and acres of flooded land. "Federal disaster," I thought to myself, wondering how I'd missed it in the newspapers, little knowing that what I was seeing was one the state's biggest cash crops—rice.

I was single and alone—except for my two dogs and my younger sister who'd moved with me—in a new place. Luckily, Little Rock is a small and friendly city, a supportive community, and distinctly Southern. The surrounding countryside—rolling green hills, rivers, and stands of pine trees—makes it a place where people enjoy the outdoors, fishing for bass and hunting duck and deer. Little Rock is home to barbeques, parties, and easy hospitality, and each person I met introduced me to someone new in turn. I made friends quickly, many of them lasting ones. The city, too, seemed bursting with talented people of my generation, full of energy and ideas: Bill Clinton was governor and his wife, Hillary, a hot lawyer in town.

I was just beginning my third decade of life. I was looking forward to launching my career, to having my first real job. I was determined to try to make my mark in television.

But the gap between the self-confidence I displayed professionally in the outside world and how I truly felt about myself inside remained unchanged. I was still an insecure damsel in distress, praying for a courageous knight to rescue her.

Be careful what you wish for.

❦

It was, on the surface at least, the stuff that movies are made of, a whirlwind courtship. I met the man who would be my husband through a friend who was a local television anchor. It was September, just a few months after I arrived in Little Rock. I was told he was a successful entrepreneur—at the time, even the word implied a kind of special cachet and daring—and he seemed, at lunch, to have nice manners and a confident, easy smile. He was also very well dressed.

When I got home later that day, there was a beautifully wrapped package on my doorstep and, inside of it, a bottle of very expensive perfume. A while later, he called to see if I had found the package and, well-brought-up girl from Fort Wayne that I was, I allowed as how the gift was way too extravagant to accept from someone I hardly knew.

Of course, I managed not to leave it at that. I went on, blurting out that I wasn't used to being given such expensive gifts.

Without missing a beat, he answered, "If you're not used to getting wonderful gifts, then the men in your life haven't been treating you right."

I kept the perfume and, without thinking, breathed a sigh of relief.

⌛

I married my second husband just two months after I met him. Looking back, I realize he insinuated himself into my life almost immediately, inviting himself to family gatherings and making plans for the two of us. In small ways and large, he took charge of my life and, frankly, I was grateful. If it wasn't true love or grand passion, it was shelter, comfort, and direction, and we became a couple because he made us one. I was flattered that a man as apparently sophisticated and worldly as he was—he wore beautiful Turnbull & Asser shirts, drove a jazzy black BMW, drank Diet Pepsi out of Waterford tumblers, worked in exquisitely appointed surroundings—wanted and loved me.

I thought his approval of me was a measure of my worth.

He proposed over burgers and beers at Shorty Small's, a well-known local joint that was the perfect foil for a grandiose gesture right out of a romance novel. He pulled a jeweler's brown evelope out of his pocket and dropped a perfect, unset three-and-a-half-carat diamond in front of me on the red-and-white checkered plastic tablecloth. I'd never seen a stone that big or that glittery blue-white. "Will you marry me?" he asked, adding that I could have the diamond set any way I liked. I don't even remember saying "yes" but I must have, the stone clasped in my hand the way a child holds a treasured object.

My engagement ring—the big stone flanked by smaller ones set in platinum—was proof positive of how much he loved me.

He seemed self-assured in every way that I didn't, and I felt safe and protected in his presence. Without ever realizing it consciously, I simply surrendered whatever independence I had and left everything up to him. He planned and arranged every detail of our wedding from the invitations to the country club, the menu, and the band. All I did was buy my dress—a long, full-skirted dotted swiss designed by Laura Ashley—that, with my hair swept up and off my face and, crowned with fresh flowers, made me look the way I felt: like a princess who'd finally been rescued by a knight in shining armor.

It all looked picture-perfect. In front of a hundred guests, I walked down the aisle on my father's arm to begin a new life, holding a tumbling spray of white lilies and star jasmine.

My two dogs in tow, I moved into his house, a two-story red brick with a deep back yard filled with pine trees. It seems to me now that those magnificent Arkansas pines were a metaphor for the marriage I had chosen for myself. While tall and majestic, they are shallow-rooted trees, only lightly anchored in the dry soil; their stature belies their fragility. During the years I lived in the house, after a storm had passed I would always go out to check if any had fallen. Sometimes, with the yard's shallow soil flooded, they had.

The house was beautifully furnished with good furniture with clean lines, all in blues, creams, and whites, with curtains that pooled onto the floor. It was another testament to his impeccable taste and style, and I didn't change or add a thing. Although I didn't see it at the time, he simply made space for me in his life and, for my part, without thinking, I moved into the space he created for me.

Only years later did I realize that the house had been designed by a professional, and that my husband had done little more than hire the right help and pay the bills. Only then did I understand that I had married someone I never really took the time to know. Living on the surface, I never looked below it.

In those first heady years, life was sweet. I loved my work and our life, and it looked as if all the dreams I'd dreamed in Fort Wayne—and even a few I hadn't— were all going to come true. In the early 1980s, Little Rock was, among other things, a lot of fun; there were tons of parties and charity functions and all sorts of reasons to get dressed up. I had a closet full of long gowns that made me feel beautiful and, at the same time, very adult and sophisticated. We were, in the beginning, invited everywhere, because of my husband—or so I thought. It never occurred to me that I might have been invited on my own merits.

We lived well because my husband believed, if he believed in anything at all, in getting the best. I was making a very good salary, particularly for Little Rock, and while my husband was characteristically vague about what he did in his office every day, there were real estate deals, a chain of hair salons, and other transactions I never paid any attention to. Looking back, I see there was a whole lot I didn't pay attention to. I handed over my paychecks and he paid the mortgage and the bills, just the way my father had handled the family finances when I was growing up. That my husband was not my father and that this was perhaps unwise—an understatement, if there ever was one—never once occurred to me.

In time, my husband's management of things, which had first seemed so appealing, became increasingly about control. My family voiced concerns about how he had me on a very short leash. Were we, they wondered, living beyond our means?

Slowly things began to unravel, bit by bit. Our social life ground to a halt—there were suddenly more parties we weren't invited to than ones we were—and our circle of friends got smaller and smaller. I felt the exclusion but didn't understand it. I didn't realize that the man I'd married had worn out his welcome and that what I took for confidence was, in other people's eyes, the swagger of pretense.

As I always had, in times of trouble, I looked away. I let my career in medicine and my growing involvement in television distract me. We adopted Kate and whatever emptiness I felt in my heart was filled by her presence. In my marriage, though, I began to feel more and more isolated, shut out, although I really didn't understand why.

I didn't have the guts or the self-awareness to confront my husband about the disintegration of our relationship. At night, I'd toss and turn, trying to imagine the future.

Then two things happened just a day apart, as, on the road of life, things sometimes do.

I came home from a medical meeting to find my husband distraught. We had an urgent problem, he said. A business deal had gone sour and he needed cash, immediately. We had, he told me, nothing in reserve, and for the first time since we'd married, I let myself begin to ask the question: Where had all the money gone?

This was, he assured me, a temporary setback, and

in a show of solidarity, I took my engagement ring off my finger and told him he could sell it. We would, I said, weather this together and, perhaps, it would make our marriage stronger.

The same evening, the other shoe dropped. A man I had never heard of called me while my husband and I were discussing Kate's fund in the kitchen. Nancy Snyderman? the voice asked, shaky and distressed. My husband was having an affair with his wife. What did I plan on doing about it?

Amazingly, I managed to get off the phone in one piece. I even mumbled something about getting back to him although, of course, I never did. My heart sank at my husband's unflustered answer, delivered in the self-confident tone I'd once so admired. The woman was a friend, just a friend, and having terrible problems in her marriage. She was depressed and so, to cheer her up, on his last trip out of town, he'd invited her along. He'd even bought her a first-class ticket and booked her a room in the same hotel he was staying in.

How very nice.

For once, I managed to keep my mouth shut. I didn't know exactly what kind of trouble I was in but I knew I was in deep. First thing in the morning, I did what millions of women do when they find themselves in way over their heads: I called my mother. Her advice was simple. First, get the ring back; you may need the money. Second, go to the safety deposit box and take a look around.

And so I did. And in that gray metal box I found evidence of another life I knew nothing about, one very different from the well-decorated world I thought I lived in, where our daughter slept peacefully in a pink-wallpapered room under the gables and the four dogs and the two cats romped in the yard. Receipts for lavish gifts I'd never been given. Reams of unpaid bills. Credit card accounts I'd never known we'd opened, all with enormous balances. An empty stock account. Threatening letters from the IRS.

We weren't just broke but deeply, deeply in debt.

And I was scared out of my wits.

⟡

The marriage was over, but getting out of it was easier said than done. At the suggestion of my lawyer—a brilliant woman who would in time become America's First Lady—I was to bide my time in the marriage while we sorted through all the financial consequences. I remember sitting with one of her colleagues, a tax attor-ney who, as I told my tale of woe, sat there with a bemused, if kind, look on his face. "Are you smiling," I asked, "because of how incredibly stupid and naive I was?" "No," he replied in a slow, Southern cadence. "I'm smiling because if I had a dime for every woman who came in with a problem like this one, I'd be a very, very rich man."

Divorce is, and was then, the leading cause of significant changes in a woman's economic status and, in the United States, the primary cause for pushing women and their children below the poverty line. While the details of what happened to me are unique (and while my earning power as a physician sets me apart from many women), the basic outlines of what happened are not unusual at all. Women surrender their independence, their ability to make informed choices, in large ways and small all the time, so that, in the traditional scheme of things they can be "taken care of." In a good relationship based in partnership—such as the one my parents have enjoyed for roughly half a century—there's nothing wrong with trusting your partner. It is only when the relationship is based in something less than true partnership—it's hard to get the image of those shallow-rooted Arkansas pines out of my head—that the choices we have made for ourselves may sometimes have enormous consequences.

In the end, I lost just about everything except the clothes on my back, my daughter, and my ex-husband's

BMW—a small act of revenge—which I paid off with a loan from my parents. The $20,000 they loaned me was seed money for a new life. I had worked for five years at a terrific salary and had literally nothing to show for it; I was thirty-five years old and on my own again, this time with a child. My husband moved to another state and I was left to deal with the debris alone. Of all the things I'd dreamed of back in Fort Wayne, the combination of a second failed marriage and going broke was not among them.

It was a shattering, humiliating, and sobering experience. I had to sell the house to meet our obligations, and the day of the closing an IRS agent was there to meet me at the title company. The proceeds from the sale literally went right into the government's outstretched hand. I had nothing left. It was a beautiful day in the South, the air fresh and scented by the azaleas and dogwoods in blossom, and surely the lowest point in my life.

Kate and I moved to a small rental house near the hospital, while I tried to figure out where to go next.

When I ricocheted out of this marriage into a disastrous relationship with yet another man I designated as knight and caretaker, I filled my bookshelves with every self-help book ever published on the subject of love and relationships. It finally took the wise words of a loving but blunt-spoken friend, Connie, who, listening to my complaints about why I was always chosen by the wrong men, reminded me that I wasn't exactly a passive participant in the psychodrama of my life.

"Maybe," she said wisely, "you need to figure out why *you* keep choosing *them.*"

⁓

What happened to me finally forced me to act. Hitting rock bottom does give you a pretty clear, if very painful, perspective on yourself.

I had to stop looking away from the problems in my life. From my late teenage years forward, my way of dealing with trouble, any kind of trouble, was to focus my attention elsewhere (usually my career) and pray that the problem would go away. I don't think that makes me very unusual; most of us find, as adults, that we all have unfinished business hanging around in the corners of our lives. In his wonderful book *The Road Less Traveled*, Dr. M. Scott Peck makes the important point that, while most of us will do just about anything to avoid dealing with a problem, "Problems call forth our courage and our wisdom; indeed, they create our courage and our wisdom. It is only because of problems that we grow mentally and spiritually."

By looking away, I hadn't permitted my failures—

particularly those of love and relationship—to teach me anything. While I had been bruised by my experiences, I hadn't grown as a result of them. And strangely enough, by cutting myself off from the learning that comes from confronting failure, I had, equally, cut myself off from the earned self-worth that comes from acknowledging success. My professional successes coexisted with deep feelings of inadequacy.

Because I hadn't let life help me grow—with the exception of the profound feelings of connection motherhood had awakened in me—inside there was still a trapped adolescent.

It was time, at the age of thirty-five, to grow up.

∽∾

Growing up, unfortunately, isn't about anything as easy or automatic as getting chronologically older. As Dr. Peck notes, moving from childhood to adulthood is more like a leap than a step and it is, in his words, "a leap that many people never really take in their lifetimes. Though they may outwardly appear to be adults, even successful adults, perhaps the majority of 'grown-ups' remain until their death psychological children who have never truly separated themselves from their parents and the power their parents have over them." Growing up involves taking risks and daring, as Dr. Peck puts it, to take charge of one's own destiny.

Growing up means having the courage to develop your own set of expectations for your life and your own definitions of "worth," not those of your parents, your spouse, or even those of society. It means being able to take care of yourself because you care *for* yourself.

Some of us grow up in adolescence but not all of us do, and I learned that year in Little Rock that, in the end, it's less important when you grow up than that you make sure you actually do.

As Dr. Peck wisely tells us, until we take the "leap into the unknown of selfhood," none of us is truly free to grow spiritually or to love fully. He puts it simply: "As long as one marries, enters a career or has children to satisfy one's parents or the expectations of anyone else, including society as a whole, the commitment by its very nature will be a shallow one."

In my own journey, doing the work of growing up came late, but not too late. In the end, I would leave Little Rock behind, finally grown-up, having learned much from the bittersweet years there and the example of the shallow-rooted pines. I would move on, finally being free to create a different kind of life, a committed one, with deeper roots.

Into the
Labyrinth

࿇

IN THE COURSE of the journey, some among us will lose the way. The year my second marriage cracked and then crumbled, I found myself in a place where every possible pathway out seemed just a blind alley leading nowhere. I was trapped in my own loneliness, an emotional prisoner in my skin, and each night, I'd lie in bed, sleepless, trying to imagine my way out. I couldn't. I had, at last, been cornered.

Ancient myth had a name for this dark testing

place of the soul: the labyrinth. At the labyrinth's center, the Minotaur, half-man, half-beast, was hidden, symbolizing the unconfronted, the truth we cannot bear to witness but that each of us needs to know. As myth had it, the way to the center where the truth is hidden is tortuous, hard, and fraught with peril. The one true path to the center is disguised by blind alleys and blocked passageways and only by holding a silver thread, symbolic of wisdom, does the hero safely make his way in and then out again.

By braving the darkness of the labyrinth's heart, by claiming the knowledge hidden at its center, and then by finding his way out into the light, back through the labyrinthine paths, the hero emerges fully whole.

As alone and trapped as I felt, I was still in the company of women. And there were two of them, each a sister of heart, who offered the silver threads I desperately needed.

∞

My terrible loneliness didn't turn me inward nor did the chaos of my life force me to look within. Instead, I looked away: Old habits die hard. I became the life of the party, the always available bartender for every occasion. I was starved for affection, and any kind of attention—even if it was the kind that was focused on someone who was drinking too much, laughing too loudly, and trying way too hard to be attractive to men—felt better than the nothing I felt when I was alone.

I was careening, and even the comfort my professional life had always offered me—the self-affirmation the white coat bestowed, the recognition from television—wasn't really working.

And it was my friend Connie who finally sat me down and painfully, carefully, and honestly told me what I was doing to myself. She'd taken me to a pancake house—there were truckers in one booth nearby, nuns in another—so that no one we knew could overhear us. Had I noticed, she asked, "that people were uncomfortable around me?" "Did I see that my friends were falling away, one by one?" "Did I realize how destructive my behavior was to myself?" The things she said were things that should have been obvious to me but weren't until I heard the words out loud. I was that lost.

In retrospect, what is truly extraordinary is that I was able to hear her at all. That I didn't contradict her or deny the truth of what she was saying or even get up from the table and walk away when she told me I needed professional help. And that I didn't crumple up the piece of paper she handed me, the one with the therapist's name and number.

Instead, I kissed her on the cheek and took the silver thread, the lifeline, she offered me. In no small measure, she helped save my life.

I'd always seen therapy as an admission of weakness, a sign that you couldn't quite manage things on your own, a failure of will or strength. I guess I also saw it as a type of self-indulgence, a New York City kind of thing out of a Woody Allen movie: lying on a couch, twice a week for years on end, talking about yourself, getting nowhere. I was wrong on both counts.

The first step toward healing is the admission that you can't, for the moment, go it alone. The second step is understanding that admitting you can't go it alone and getting help for yourself aren't signs of weakness but of resilience. Thinking yourself worthy of saving, of help, of change, is the beginning of the path. The final step is understanding fully and honestly that becoming whole is a process, not a lesson learned in hours or days. I still consider myself a work-in-progress.

Becoming whole, as the myth of the labyrinth tells us, is an inward journey.

The modest little office in a nondescript building on the streets of Little Rock, up a narrow flight of stairs and through a small reception room with just a few chairs and some magazines, belied how important what went on there would be for the rest of my life. Therapy began to peel away layer after layer of self-doubt and rationalization that had made me feel, for most of my adult life, uncomfortable in my skin. It was a new experience for me, speaking aloud to an impartial observer, someone who had no expectations of me or for me. I had assumed he'd know Dr. Nancy Snyderman from television—Little Rock is a small place, after all—but if he did, he never let on. In his eyes, what I did in the world was of little import; I was simply a person in need of help.

In the confines of that room, in the quiet, I could begin to listen to myself, hear my own words, and recognize the parts of me that were valuable and worthy. I began to see myself as a human being, as a woman, more than just the sum of my accomplishments in the world.

I began, slowly, to comprehend that I had to try to live according to my own expectations, not anyone else's. I had let myself get so caught up in how other people saw me that I had little sense of how I saw myself. In a very real way, I had lost sight not only of myself but of what mattered to me. As he put it, simply and wisely, "What the world thinks of me is none of my business."

Therapy was both a process of learning and unlearning. I had never chosen to be alone willingly—solitude was, I thought, a synonym for loneliness—and throughout my adult life, when I had found myself alone, I'd always filled the silence with distractions by turning the television on or playing music. Instead, my therapist encouraged me to listen to the silence and to meditate, a practice I still turn to when I am troubled or simply world-weary. I learned to spend time by myself and discovered that those quiet times of solitary thought were moments of renewal. I began, bit by bit, to take the time to get to know myself and discovered, in the process, new aspects of selfhood.

To help journey farther inward, to get below the surface of my conscious thoughts and connections, my therapist suggested hypnosis. And despite my initial skepticism, I found it invaluable, a way of getting out of the "now" of time and place and fully, really, relaxing and letting go. Lying on the couch in that office, with my therapist's help, I felt quiet and at peace. The defenses of the body and psyche relax under hypnosis; it feels like nothing less than shedding a full coat of heavy armor, and rediscovering your own lightness. Your body literally quiets down—your heart rate and respiration drop—and you enter an open space where you can hear your own voice. These sessions left me energized and feeling positive, armed with a sense of confidence that came from a deeper, more rooted place than any other feeling I'd had before.

At the center of my labyrinth, I discovered a woman who had more imagination and depth than I had imagined. And, on the whole, I liked her.

But therapy was only the first step. Therapy opens the door, but it is up to the patient to walk through it. My journey toward both emotional wellness and wholeness was just only beginning; I was still at the labyrinth's center.

What still eluded me was an essential groundedness, a sense of purpose and meaning in my life—apart from the things I did for others—that went beyond the surface of things. There had been just a few moments when I had caught a glimpse of what, I thought, might be the hand of God at work—chief among them the phone call that night that brought Kate into my life— but moored as I was in the day-to-day, there was little room for spirit in my life.

A special place and the example of yet another extraordinary friend would change all that.

~∞~

The journey out of the labyrinth's center took me into unfamiliar territory, both literally and symbolically. A group of Kellogg Fellows, of whom I was one, decided to attend a workshop on spirituality in Taos, New Mexico, which filled me with more than a little trepidation. For one thing, I recognized some very real differences between myself and the other members of the group. They seemed further along in understanding, more together in important ways, more evolved some-how. I didn't exactly know what went on in a spirituali-ty workshop but I figured, if the others thought it was a good thing, it probably was.

Chief among those I admired was Diana. I was, from the first, drawn to her because of our differences. Brilliant and intellectual—she was then a professor and is now the president of Wellesley College—her habits of mind were the opposite of mine, and she seemed to know intuitively what I struggled to learn. She was and is eager to look below the surface and quick to point out the important connections between events and people that, to other eyes including mine, would seem totally unrelat-ed. She was, I thought, cut from a finer, rarer cloth than I, and I looked up to her. She is also a person of confirmed faith, conscious of the role spirit plays in her life.

And by learning from her, I was able to grasp the other silver thread I needed.

Looking back, I don't think it was an accident that I found myself in Taos at the same time in my life that I had begun to work my way out of the labyrinth.

෴

Taos has a magic of its own. Just being in the extra-ordinary landscape that is New Mexico began to open up my soul, for this is country that holds thousands of years of sacred history within its breast. I felt it first in the ruins of the pueblos where the spirits of the Anasazi—their name means "the ancient ones" in Navajo—seemed not just to animate the place but the faces and gestures of their descendants, the Pueblo Indians. It is said that they came to the valley with the help of an eagle spirit-guide. Taos is a place where the distinction between earth and heaven are blurred. For centuries, series of villages were built facing the sacred mountains, now called the Sangre de Cristo. The range takes its Spanish name—"the blood of Christ"—from how it looks each evening, bathed red in the light of the setting sun.

I didn't know it when I set out, but Taos and the areas surrounding it have changed many, many lives. They are all places where people have come to find a simpler, more connected way of life, artists and writers among them. It was at Taos that the American artist Georgia O'Keeffe first discovered the stark beauty of the desert, and the vision that allowed her to see the sacred, the permanent, and the universal in the ordinary detail: the dried bones of cattle, the lines of a single flower. The English writer and poet D. H. Lawrence, who lived in and is buried in Taos, wrote, "I think that New Mexico was the greatest experience from the outside world that

I have ever had. It certainly changed me forever. . . . the moment I saw the brillant, proud morning shine high up over the deserts of Santa Fe, something stood still in my soul, and I started to attend."

I love those words—"something stood still in my soul, and I started to attend." They remind me now of what I first learned, with some difficulty, in Taos: What the spirit needs is always around us. We simply need to attend and listen.

I began to learn to listen at Taos but, once again, it did not come easily. Our workshop leader and facilitator, Parker Palmer, an author, poet, and educator, encouraged us to sit in a circle, share our experiences, and open up to spirit. I sat there, feeling very much on the fringes, as though the associations the others were making were somehow beyond me. Questions of spirit and soul had never been at the center of my life and, try as I might, I couldn't make the connection. Then he asked us to go off alone, to meditate and write poetry. I froze. Being alone by choice was still so new to me that I was instantly uncomfortable. What was I supposed to write about? I honestly didn't feel as if I had anything to say. I literally begged Diana to come off and talk with me instead. Why be alone when you can spend time with a friend? Besides, I was a doctor and a scientist, not an artist or a teacher, and I didn't write poetry.

To my surprise, Diana quietly and simply told me I needed to try to do the work. Even though we lived hundreds of miles apart, the direction my life had taken, the accumulation of bad choices and judgments, had not escaped her attention. She was as concerned as my friend Connie had been about the way I was living, though her take on what was happening to me was a little different. This was the work I needed to do, she thought; perhaps, just perhaps, the inner spirit was the piece of self that was missing. With her encouragement and her company, I felt secure enough to try.

And I did. I took being alone baby-step by baby-step, and began to let myself listen to what the landscape and the group had to teach me. I literally journeyed alone into the canyons of Taos, taking in the earth and sky, and then came back and began to write. I put aside worries about whether the poems were good or bad, or whether they measured up to the words of my fellow travelers; I simply wrote.

The act of putting pen to paper—my thoughts and feelings being given shape on the page—gave me another way of seeing myself. I experienced a measure of clarity about myself and my place in the world, a different kind of connectedness. The spirit of Taos demanded that I take a deep breath, and in breathing deep, I realized I hadn't taken the time to breathe in some important way for months, maybe even years, on end. I slowed down despite myself. Amid the brilliant contrasts of the New Mexico landscape, clear and without distraction—mountains etched against sky and then against the rocky plateau—I saw myself as part of something larger and heard, for the first time, the echoes of the earth and sky in the rhythms of my own heart. That sense of something larger—it doesn't matter if you call it God or simply a pattern that gives meaning to human existence—allowed me to make a commitment to myself. I resolved to begin my journey anew, this time soulfully and mind-fully.

The last time I was in Taos, to celebrate my fortieth birthday, much had changed in my life, and the turmoil of those years was, in large part, behind me. Once again, Diana was my companion that snowy March when the sacred mountains around Taos were blanketed in white, and only the wind whispered through the mountain passes. We stoked the fire and talked, read, and wrote. We spent time together and alone.

And I could still hear the voice of the earth echo in the sound of my own heartbeat.

༺༒༻

Finding my way out of the labyrinth took time and work. The lessons learned from both therapy and the spiritual journey that was Taos took time to absorb, and even longer to integrate fully into my life. I consider myself blessed that I had two friends who were there to help me find the way. I am even luckier that each of them cared enough about me to risk telling me the truth.

We need, in the circle of women, to be one another's advocates. We need to encourage one another to seek help and treatment in moments of crisis. We need to remind each other that getting help is not an act of weakness or an admission of failure but a positive, restorative step, and we must support women we know who are taking that step. We need to work on ridding society of the stigmas associated with therapy and other kinds of intervention, precisely because, as women, we are at greater risk for many mental disorders than men are. According to the National Institute of Mental Health, more than 19 million adult Americans, ages eighteen and older, will suffer from a depressive illness each year. Importantly, while 12 percent of women will be affected by a depressive disorder, only 7 percent of men will be. Similarly, anxiety disorders affect twice as many women as men.

It's only been comparatively recently—in the last two decades—that medical research has actually begun to address the meaningful differences, both physiological and emotional, between women and men, and their impact on mental health. As the National Institute of

Mental Health puts it in their valuable pamphlet "Depression: What Every Woman Should Know," the varied factors unique to women's lives contribute significantly to depression. Among these factors are the issues of adolescence (which result in eating disorders in young women but which may resurface in later life in a different form), the effect of hormones, and the changing reproductive cycle. (The distinct stages of a woman's life may render her susceptible to depression at different times, and it may take different forms such as premenstrual syndrome, postpartum depression, or depression associated with menopause.)

Precisely because women define themselves in terms of relationships, as psychologist Carol Gilligan and others have shown, changes in a woman's important relationships may contribute to the onset of depression. Not surprisingly, the rate of depression is highest among unhappily married women.

I am living proof that patterns of unhealthy behavior as well as decades-old issues of self-esteem can, with intervention and commitment, be changed. As I approach my fifth decade of life, I look back at these times of turmoil and, in a way, I am thankful they happened. I wouldn't have gotten where I am today if I hadn't gotten fully lost in the labyrinth first, a necessary journey. Finding myself there and then getting myself out were the true beginnings of a better life.

There is a wonderful quotation that says it all better than I can, written in the early years of the twentieth century by writer Mary Antin:

> We are not born all at once, but by bits. The body first, and the spirit later; and the birth and growth of the spirit, in those who are attentive to their own inner life, slow and exceedingly painful. Our mothers are racked with the pains of our physical birth; we ourselves suffer the longer pains of our spiritual growth.

We each do give birth to our spiritual selves but we must remember that we do not need to do it alone.

An Affair
of the Heart

BECOMING WHOLE IS hard work. Nothing on this planet is born with ease. The seedling struggles up through hard earth; the chick pecks its way out of the egg; the sea turtle emerges buried in the sand and far from the water's edge; the butterfly shakes itself violently, perilously, to be freed from the prison of the chrysalis.

The birth of the true self is no easier and, like every birth, it is a process.

In the wake of my second failed marriage, I struggled to piece myself together, feeling needy and alone. Despite the magic and illumination of Taos, my therapy, and the support of my friends, I found it hard to break the old patterns. A part of me still clung to the fantasy of the knight who would make my life complete. Emergence is slow. Even as the process of therapy yanked and pulled me toward health and true adulthood, I sought comfort in a relationship based on the old patterns.

The journey teaches us to be patient with ourselves.

The relationship ended but because of it, my life took yet another turn.

∞

I discovered I was pregnant at a time when my life was at its most unsettled. I had already decided to leave Little Rock but was still working out the details of where Kate and I would live. Both San Francisco and New York were real possibilities in terms of my dual careers of medicine and television, but what precisely the future held for me in either of those two cities was, of course, unknown. My divorce was still not final. My finances were in ruins. Therapy was still an ongoing process. And my old standbys in times of trouble, would-be candidates for knights in shining armor, were—mercifully, as it happens—in very short supply.

The intersection at which I found myself —that of a single woman's unplanned pregnancy—is one so personal, so individual, that it defies all generalizations. This part of the journey isn't one where women can learn from example, and so the personal choice I made over a decade ago was and is uniquely mine, and mine alone. Each woman finds herself alone at this crossroads and must look within to find her own voice and choose her own path. The many details that distinguish one woman's life from another and render each of us a unique, sentient being at a particular stage of life make a single, right answer to the choice posed at this particular crossroads an impossibility, save one: Listen to your heart.

And listening to my heart, at the age of thirty-six, I chose to bring a child into the world on my own. My ability to make a living—the simple fact that, even alone, I could provide for the financial needs of a one-parent family—made it a hard, but realistic, choice. It was a momentous decision, one with considerable ramifications for me, the daughter I already had, and the one growing inside me. It was a choice that could be informed by the love and support of some of my friends and family but which only I could make. It was a decision that forced me finally to slough off the middle-class expectations and standards with which I'd been brought up and to replace them with expectations and commitments that were personal in every sense of the word. In doing so, I would learn, with pain and difficulty, precisely what it means and what it costs to choose your own path in a world governed by convention.

For the first time in my life, I was, in the truest sense, on my own.

Bringing a child into the world is surely the most important, life-defining choice a woman can make, and at the age of thirty-six, I thought I had few illusions about how difficult the path of single motherhood would be. But having never traveled the path, I couldn't and didn't know the unexpected ways in which it would test me, as well as bring me terrific joy, satisfaction, and strength.

This was the journey that would forge my soul and, in the end, make me whole.

⌦

Real growth is painful and difficult, and the path I took to become fully grown was tortuous.

I moved to San Francisco six months pregnant, in the summer of 1988, ready to start my life over once again. It was a city I'd chosen precisely because I had no connection to it, no old patterns to fall back into. I'd only been to San Francisco once, for a medical meeting years before, and I thought the fact that I had no history there—and no friends or even acquaintances—would mean that I could start with a clean slate. It was, friends reminded me, a cosmopolitan city filled with opportunities, a place where many people moved to find a new life. I'd lined up two jobs, one with a hospital and the other with a local television station, and had found a rental apartment in an older building—complete with high ceilings and moldings—for us to live in. I had paid the deposit on the place, wired from Little Rock, with money borrowed from a colleague.

I arrived alone in the middle of a July heat wave, while my mother watched Kate in Fort Wayne until I got settled. I remember the day I sat in the apartment's empty space, surrounded by bare white walls, waiting for the furniture to arrive from Little Rock and the phone company to hook up the lines. I felt utterly, totally alone in this unfamiliar city that was supposed to be a place for new beginnings. Scrunched in a corner of the living room, feeling more like a lost child than anything else, I drew my knees to my chest and rocked and cried.

Nothing during those months was easy except my pregnancy which was, thankfully, uneventful. The schedule of the two jobs—the hospital in the morning, a daily spot as medical correspondent on the evening news—meant that I was always on the go, and felt as if I belonged nowhere. While I'd imagined the anonymity conferred by a city to be the perfect backdrop for reinventing myself, I didn't realize how isolating city life could be. Surrounded by strangers, I found the circumstances of my life uncomfortable and embarrassing, my choices hard to explain. With my growing belly telegraphing my news to the world, it was impossible to hide inside the white coat, the familiar place I'd always withdrawn when the going got rough. The most innocent of questions—"When is your husband joining you?"—stripped away my fledgling layers of self and I found myself caught in a series of lies about a mythical about-to-arrive husband that only made me feel all the more isolated. As my due date neared, I finally gave up lying and, no other choices at hand, took a deep breath and told the truth. People were kinder than I had any right to expect.

The easy comforts of my childhood in Fort Wayne and of my life in Little Rock seemed part of someone else's distant past. I had no savings, still owed plenty, had one child to take care of and another on the way, and then discovered that I hadn't been at the television job long enough to qualify for maternity leave. My hospital salary—for just a half day's part-time work and at a significant paycut—wasn't enough for us to live on. I applied for disability and discovered that living in one of the world's most expensive cities had its price: the disability wouldn't even cover a month's rent. That pretty much settled it: no maternity leave. The loving sitter who looked after Kate while I worked would have to tend to Rachel as well.

I put on a brave face but, inside, I was forlorn, lonely, worn out from working all day and coming home to a toddler at night. Many of the defenses I'd used all of my life to bully my way through hard situations had been undone by the process of therapy, but at this point in the journey, there wasn't yet a stong enough self to function in their place. I longed for the circle of friends I'd had in Little Rock. I ached for someone to step in and take care of me.

There were many times when staying the course seemed impossible, and more than once, I found myself making plans to go back to Little Rock to find some measure of comfort. I didn't act on the impulse. Instead, I worked both jobs up to the day Rachel was born.

❧

Rachel was born healthy and safe at 1:29 in the morning on November 14, 1988, at the end of one of the nicest days I'd had since arriving in San Francisco. My mother had come in on Saturday to help me take care of Kate, and the women at the television station were throwing me a baby shower on Sunday. Even though my water broke just a few hours before the party was scheduled to start, my obstetrician thought it was fine that I went, and we planned to meet at the hospital later that day. I felt loved, wanted, and welcomed for the first time in many, many months. During the party, Eileen, one of the producers, asked me quietly if I had anyone to go through the delivery with me. I didn't, and she did me a great act of kindness by volunteering. It was comforting to check in to the hospital with someone by my side and even nicer, when it came time to push, to hold someone's hand.

I'd like to be able to say—it'd be lyrical and inspiring—that in giving birth to Rachel on my own I gave birth to myself, but it's far more complicated than that. We all look to quick fixes—the diet that lets us lose weight without feeling hungry, the exercise plan that doesn't take discipline, the loving relationship that doesn't take work—but coming into selfhood, like everything else important in human life, doesn't come in a quick-fix format. Having my daughter was just a step in a much longer, difficult process. The photographs taken at the time show a smiling thirty-something woman holding a perfect baby, but if you were to look closely, you'd see that the mother's eyes look hollow and sad, and that she's downright exhausted. A week after Rachel was born, I went back to work at both jobs, racing back to the apartment to breast-feed, pumping my breasts in between.

On the surface, it looked good: I was working hard, taking care of us financially, and paying off my debts. I talked an even better story to anyone who asked. Inside, though, I was totally disheartened, adrift, and terribly lonely. How *do* you make a life for yourself? I hadn't a clue. I had acquaintances at work, but at the end of the day in a city of commuters, they went home, back to their lives, while I went back to my apartment.

And so, reverting to old ways once more, I decided to move back to Little Rock. I was going "home" to a place where life wouldn't be so damn hard. I'd get my old job back, I thought, and start fresh. I called my parents with my news and my father rightly, wisely told me it wouldn't work. "You want to step back into your old life again and pick up where you left off, without all the turmoil,' he said. "Life doesn't work that way."

Of course, I was sure he was wrong. I flew to Little Rock and found a house in a beautiful old section I'd never lived in before and actually made an offer on it. I went to the university to try to get my appointment back only to discover—to no one's surprise except mine—

that life in Little Rock had moved on. No job. And without the financial means, I was forced back to San Francisco.

Once again, someone must have been watching over me. Being forced to stay the course was a blessing in disguise.

༄

And the busy rhythms of the days and weeks of my life in San Francisco moved me forward. I devoted myself to my girls and my work and, for the first time, I made the conscious decision to stay single and unattached. I'd spent almost two decades of my so-called adulthood thinking that I existed as a woman only by being part of a couple. By choosing solitude—the small circle of family that was me and my girls—I was finally able to let go of the fantasy of the knight in shining armor for once and all. I was able to learn how choosing to be alone permits you to love for reasons other than simple loneliness.

The solitary path I'd chosen taught me a great deal about the importance and meaning of relationship in my life. I'd always looked toward the relationship I had with a man as the primary source of my definition as a woman. Now, without a man in my life, I had to look elsewhere for meaning and connection. The new commitment I had made to a life on my own with my children reshaped how I understood and valued the relationships that were a part of my life and permitted me, in time, to envision a relationship with a man that wasn't about caretaking but about partnership.

Thrust into my own company, I began to like myself and to trust my own heart, not just on occasion but most of the time. On my own, I learned to listen to myself and, for the first time, to learn fully from the necessary journey.

The path I'd chosen threw the important relationships in my life into high relief. I recognized how important women were to my life, and how my definition of myself depended as much on the love that comes out of friendship as anything else. There were the close women friends who understood my need to talk while they listened. While they had made different choices in their lives than I, they never questioned my need to choose alone. The questions they asked me were the questions I needed to answer, and to this day I can never thank them enough for the safe haven they gave me in a time of tremendous upheaval and change. For the last decade, being in the circle of women has allowed me to draw on reserves of strengths I did not know I had and made me the beneficiary of collective wisdom based in other women's experiences.

I discovered, too, that the circle of women was not

just made up of longtime intimates and old friends. The biology women share is most visible, most accessible, during pregnancy, and the small acts of kindness offered me by acquaintances and sometimes strangers helped me on the way, and assuaged my feelings of loneliness. In the years since, sharing both the trials and satisfactions that make up motherhood with other women has offered unexpected but pleasurable moments of insight, growth, and connection.

While pregnancy and childbirth had never been a part of how I thought I would define myself as a woman, I realized that the experience of pregnancy did make me feel a part of the eternal rhythms of the world and the lives of all the women who had given birth before me. There is a sense in which every woman gives birth on her own, and it was my mother who reminded me that what I was doing was just what women had done since the dawn of human history. I gained a new spiritual history I hadn't had before, a new sense of belonging, and a different perspective on my own life.

Just as the experience of finding Kate and taking her into my arms and heart had changed the boundaries of who I was as a person, so, too, the experience of carrying Rachel on my own transformed my sense of who I was and what I needed. I was emotionally enriched by the depth of my commitments to my children, commitments more profound than any I'd mustered in any of my relationships with men, even the two I'd married. Years later, at the next stage of my life, bearing a child in the context of committed and adult love would teach me still other lessons.

By taking care of us, I learned to care for me. And through these acts of caring, I became, over time, a woman of substance.

∽∾

Weathering this painful and trying part of the journey—living through it, rather than bolting from it as I had every other time of crisis—changed me in large ways and small. I learned, for one thing, a measure of patience and a great deal about the process of growth: There was no single, pivotal moment when things in my life suddenly fell into place. Instead, it was more a series of little steps that, in the end, amounted to great strides. I grew into my own by learning to articulate my own expectations, setting my own standards, rather than relying on others to supply them for me. Finding meaning and satisfaction in my day-to-day life without a partner allowed me to imagine a different kind of relationship than any I'd either stumbled into or sought out.

Once again, the wise Dr. Peck puts my own experience into a larger context. Pain, as he points out, appears to be part of the very process of maturation, and, in his words, "Many people are either unwilling or unable to suffer the pain of giving up the outgrown which needs to be forsaken. Consequently they cling, often forever, to their old patterns of thinking and behaving, thus failing to negotiate any crisis, to truly grow up, and to experi- ence the joyful sense of rebirth that accompanies the suc- cessful transition into greater maturity."

His phrase—"the joyful sense of rebirth"— resounds with meaning. Simply living through the expe- rience of those first years—the equal drudgery and chal- lenge of taking care of myself and my two small chil- dren—and managing to come out the other side imbued me with a sense of confidence and independence which, finally, blurred the boundaries between my inner and outer selves.

But there's another lesson of value here. It wasn't simply that I needed to learn independence; I had to learn to be independent in the context of relationship.

While Dr. Peck's work speaks to both the experi- ences of men and women, there is a sense in which this part of the journey toward true adulthood—the neces- sary crisis—may be different for women. The ground- breaking work of Dr. Carol Gilligan, detailed in her book *In a Different Voice* almost twenty years ago, demonstrated that there were significant differences in how girls and boys and, later, women and men define themselves and perceive the role of relationship in their lives. Boys and men define themselves through their autonomy and aloneness. Male identity proceeds from separation and, then, from locating the self on a hierarchical ladder of achievement. Girls and women, on the other hand, focus on relationship as the major part of defining themselves. In Dr. Gilligan's words, "In their portrayal of relationships, women replace the bias of men toward separation with a representation of the interdependence of self and other, both in love and work."

The male model for the journey toward selfhood is the hero on a quest who forges himself by being alone. In fairy tale and story—some of it ancient and some of it contemporary—the only female counterpart to the loner knight is the passive princess, Sleeping Beauty or Cinderella, who looks to the hero for her awakening. Dr. Gilligan's findings, as well as those of her colleagues, suggest that the male model isn't applicable to a woman's necessary journey. Just going it alone will not get us where we need to go.

And so it was in my experience. As a woman, it wasn't simply living alone that permitted my growth but living alone *with* my children. When I let go of the narrow definition of "relationship"—that of the man who would make me whole—I freed myself to look at all the other relationships in my life as places of meaning and affirmation. The self I saw reflected in all of those connections, the web of relationships that made up my life—my roles as mother, friend, sister, daughter, doctor and television correspondent, colleague and coworker, neighbor—was a woman of complexity, made strong by the variety and range of her emotional commitments.

Instead of seeing the emphasis women put on relationship and interconnection as a weakness, we need to understand and value it as a strength. Once we look past our largely adolescent notions of rescuing, romantic love as the only place of definition, we can focus on all the myriad connections we make in our lives and begin to understand them as true sources of inspiration, wellsprings for our sense of self.

And, then, perhaps, in one another's company, we will discover that we already own the keys to the kingdom.

A Single Step

❦

IN THAT BEAUTIFUL city by the bay, I watched with pleasure and amazement as my children grew. Green-eyed, blond Rachel emerged from infancy to become a round-faced smiling toddler, full of beans, while my dark-haired, brown-eyed Kate's amazing expressiveness (she'd been talking since the age of nine months!) filled me with wonder. And our busy but stable life nurtured my spirit. I remember sitting in the living room early in the morning and then alone at night, when my girls were fast asleep, by the windows that looked out onto the beauty of the Golden Gate Bridge and San Francisco Bay. I felt, for the first time in my adult life, centered and grounded; the impetuousness that had marked so many of my personal decisions had given way to something different.

The view out of those windows—the Golden Gate, the marina, the distant edge of Marin county and all that lay beyond it, and, on the clearest days, the outlines of the Bay Bridge—helped me, a Midwestern girl at heart, get used to life in a crowded city. The view was the yard and the open space I didn't have four floors up, and it reminded me of the larger world outside the little one the three of us lived in. I would watch as the fog rolled in, sometimes hiding the bridge entirely in its pillowy grip and then, at other times, looking more like lacy wisps that magically floated above and below the bridge's red-orange lines. In the mornings, bathed in the northern light, the marina glowed softly, as if burnished by an artist's brush, while the bridge seemed almost to boast of its fiery color. At night, the bridge's lights made it look like a shimmering pearl necklace flung into the dark.

In front of those windows, I felt whole, though surely I missed the comfort and joy of an intimate relationship. But the view also let me imagine a future that might lie beyond the confines of the moment. It wasn't a future I was actively seeking; it was simply that I began, slowly, to believe in its possibility.

There's a wonderful passage in the *Tao te Ching*, written probably 2,300 years ago, which describes where I was then and where I thought I might someday go: "The tree which fills the arms grew from the tiniest sprout; the tower of nine stories rose from a small heap of earth; the journey of a thousand miles commenced with a single step."

⌒∞⌒

Improbably, it all started with a dress. I guess if a love story, any love story—even one with, say, Ingrid Bergman and Cary Grant in luminous black and white—starts with a dress, it must be a beyond-your-dreams, utterly fabulous dress. It should probably cost more than you can afford, and in this instance, it did. I bought the dress—an extravagant floor-length gown with a dropped-waist velvet top, taffeta skirt, and sleeves embroidered with silver thread, bugle beads, and pearls—because I was being photographed for a book called *Gifted Woman* by Howard Schatz. I'm not sure why I was chosen to be in it—it featured California women and I hardly qualified as a Californian—but it turned out to be important in a way I never expected.

Because the photographer knew I rode horses, his idea was to have me dressed to the nines, holding the reins of a magnificent black thoroughbred. And that is actually how he photographed me, with the coastal town of Bolinas as a backdrop, looking not at all like myself but like an elegant princess from a mystical kingdom, a vision in black. It was the little girl in me playing dress-up, and I loved every moment of it.

After the photograph was taken, the dress hung in my closet because I had nowhere to wear it and no one in particular to wear it for. The dress became the perfect excuse to throw a Christmas party. I didn't know too many people—just a few from the hospital and television station—but I did have the dress. I told everyone to wear whatever they wanted and, since it was San Francisco, they took me at my word. A woman I knew from the television station asked if she could bring a single colleague—she planned on fixing him up with another friend who'd also been invited—and I said, "Sure, why not?" The more, the merrier.

The atmosphere was festive—the Christmas tree was up and decorated in the living room—and in the distance, the glittering lights of the bridge and the marina looked as if they'd been strung in the night sky just for me and my guests.

The man in the blue jeans and leather jacket was

blond, terrifically handsome, and, I thought, a bit younger than I. He introduced himself when I greeted him at the door. He was a sports producer at the station I worked at, though our paths had never crossed. It didn't take me long to find out how old he was (five years younger than I was) and to remind him, at my flirtatious best (fortified by the black dress, after all), that he wasn't too young for me. (A bit more subtle, I guess, than "I'm not too old for you.") I mixed with my guests, but Doug was the last to leave. When he kissed me good-bye, he asked if he could see me on New Year's Day.

We celebrated the first day of 1991 in each other's company.

∾

But for the first time in my life, I was committed to taking it slow. Doug was still very bruised from his own divorce (he had been suddenly and ruthlessly discarded) and I wasn't ready to change the life I'd built with my two girls. In single motherhood, I had finally come into my own, and I was the least selfish and most focused I'd ever been. Now that I didn't need rescuing, I finally understood that making a man a part of my life was an active choice, and I gave myself and the girls the opportunity to get to know him and for him to know us.

It had taken a hell of a long time but I was finally grown up.

He was—and is—kind, smart, athletic, and fun, and the two of us together are a study in balance. He brings quiet to my boisterousness, while his habits of mind—he is analytical and a careful decision-maker—temper my quick, off-the-cuff, and sometimes, still, impetuous spirit. He has a wry sense of humor that suits me just fine. Most important, perhaps for no reason more complicated than that he worked in television himself and was gifted at it (the Emmys in our house belong to him, not me), he wasn't fazed, distracted, or even terrifically impressed by my work on TV. (In his words, people on television are just that: people . . . on television. He knows that the people behind the camera are the ones who work hardest, even though the credit goes to those in front of it.) He maintained, as he does to this day, that my being a doctor is and should be the anchor of my professional life. Over the next two years and then some, we saw more and more of each other—skiing together, going on picnics and hikes, doing ordinary things with pleasure—and gradually, the relationship took on a more committed aspect, and he became a part of the circle the children and I had formed.

And he embraced my girls and they loved him.

But I still hung back. I had, after all, two failed marriages behind me, and this time, I wanted nothing less than true partnership. Was I ready to commit to all that true partnership entailed? To learn a new path I'd never taken? At the same time, I couldn't, with my children in mind, just live with him; the next step, if we took it, would have to include marriage. For all the times I bent the rules, inside there was still the girl who grew up in Fort Wayne, Indiana, whose parents had been happily married forever, and I couldn't see my way clear to unwedded bliss.

But marriage, too, posed a quandary. My independence, the growth of my self-reliance, had been so hard fought that I wasn't sure that choosing to get married again wasn't a sign of weakness, an admission that I couldn't make it on my own. I was proud of the life I had managed to make for myself and my girls, and of the ways I had changed. But then, there was Doug himself: loving, true, and open. And I was happy with him.

I decided, for the first time in my life, to keep my own counsel, and didn't even ask the advice of the people closest to me, my girlfriends and parents. This was a decision I knew I had to make for myself, by myself.

I waited and, as I had learned to, I listened to my heart.

During the spring of 1993 the four of us had a week-long trip planned to the old whaling village of

Mendocino, first settled in the 1850s, up the Northern California coast. The village lies just below the forests of giant redwoods that spurred the logging and lumber boom that built up the town. I had started going up there with the girls, trying to establish a family tradition like the ones the family I had been born into had, renting the same little house that sits just over the dunes, and this time Doug was going with us. Mendocino is a magical place with a rugged coastline, where the Pacific waves crash over rocks high up on the cliffs. It is a varied landscape—forest, headlands, canyons, dunes, meadows, and, just up the coast, a clear ten miles of beach. The homes the lumber barons built still stand proud, and Mendocino is beautiful and weathered, a small slice of the past that seems far removed from the bustle of America at the end of the twentieth century. It is a place to relax, enjoy nature, and recharge the body and soul.

As the vacation neared, I suddenly found myself thinking about Mendocino just a bit differently. Was it hard, I wondered, to get married in Mendocino? A call to the courthouse revealed it wasn't; you didn't need a blood test, just a driver's license or passport. (California can be very laid-back, thank goodness.) I made an appointment at the Mendocino County courthouse in the Ukiah County seat. Next, I found myself buying beautiful floral mid-calf dresses for the girls. If I ended up getting cold feet, I figured they could always wear them for Easter. Three days before the trip, I marched myself into Tiffany and bought two wedding bands. I didn't engrave them—bad luck, I thought—and then my assistant, Angie, and I went ahead and ordered flowers and made reservations at Cafe Beaujolais, the best restaurant in town.

I took the girls out—Rachel was four and Kate six-and-a-half—and asked how they'd feel if Doug became a true, permanent part of our lives. They were thrilled and excited. I knew, had always known, that they needed and wanted a father but, more important, I knew I couldn't act on that alone. Everyone in the equation deserved and needed more.

Thank you, everyone—you know who you are—for teaching me to listen to my heart.

The day we were to leave, I packed an extra hang-up bag with the girls' dresses, an old but favorite plum-colored Laura Ashley dress for me, and a suit, tie, shirt, cufflinks, and shoes for Doug. (It turned out, later, that I had forgotten a belt, but never mind.) Doug asked why the hang-up bag was there— this was a hiking vacation, after all, and the other suitcases were packed with sweat clothes, shorts, and hiking boots—but I smiled and just said that maybe the girls and I would want to get dressed up for Easter.

There was only one thing I hadn't done.

I hadn't told Doug.

༄

What happened next was what my husband laughingly calls the "Easter Ambush." The air that day in April was crisp and clean in Mendocino and the four of us headed out for an evening walk on the beach. The beach on this part of the coast is beautiful and wide and dotted with driftwood; just off shore, large rocks formations jut out of the Pacific. Here, in spring, the seals come to have their pups, congregating in noisy, barking groups, while the sandpipers and other birds skitter along the shoreline's wet sand. Pools between the rocks, at low tide, shelter all manner of inhabitants. While the coast is alive with life and energy—the waves bursting onto the shoreline, then pooling and eddying—the sound of the waters also soothes the spirit. It was, I thought, the perfect place to take that first step of the journey of one thousand miles.

Rachel toddled up to Doug and told him that we had a very, very important question for him. Doug looked at me and then at Kate, who pulled the blue Tiffany box out from behind her back. He opened it, and saw the two wedding rings. There was just a tiny pause and then he said, "You want to get engaged?" I hadn't, in my wisdom, sent the clearest of messages.

As the girls shouted, "We want you to be our daddy," I told him about the appointment at the courthouse.

His eyes shone with his answer. And he swept both girls up in his arms and said, "Of course."

And after a night under the stars, sipping champagne and snacking on caviar, we were married by Brenda, the courthouse clerk, on the lawn in front of the building in the simplest of ceremonies, with the two girls, wreaths of flowers in their hair, in attendance. There were vows that each of us pledged to and that, this time, had a special resonance. Brenda was kind enough to take a picture of the four of us and, to this day, the photograph is one of my favorites. It captures a perfect moment: The four of us are standing in the meadow behind the courthouse; in the distance, you can see the blue waters of the Pacific. The two little girls are positively beaming and I look luminous, with windswept hair. Doug is smiling broadly. It is a portrait of a family with high hopes, looking toward the future together, set against a brilliant blue sky. Afterward, we all went off for a celebratory lunch where, in her loudest six-year-old voice, Kate gave the hostess the news: "This is my new dad, Doug." And with that, everyone in the restaurant joined in the party.

We returned home a married couple with two children. It was nothing, to my mind at least, short of miraculous.

My journey, from this point on, would be shared. And the view from my windows changed forever; the future was at hand.

∞

Our marriage was a surprise to friends and family—why wouldn't it be? Even the groom hadn't known!—and we wisely waited a few days to tell the world. I think we needed the time alone to let the weight and meaning of the commitment we'd made to each other and to the children sink in. Not surprisingly, the reaction we got was cautiously congratulatory. Both of our mothers gushed while our fathers were largely silent. Understandably, Doug's father expressed concern that his son had married a slightly older woman with the responsibility for two young children. My father was quiet until I asked him how he felt. His answer— it was, after all, his daughter's third time out—came in the form of a question: "Does Doug know you're not very good at this?"

And in that wonderful witticism that had us all laughing—it's a story we've told among ourselves many times over—is more than just a shred of truth. I did know that I hadn't been very good at the commitment, the hard work, that a marriage involves. Both therapy and living alone with my children had forced me to come to terms with why those earlier relationships had failed, and the measure of commitment I made to this marriage was entirely different. I was, as was my husband, determined to make it work—for ourselves, for each other, and for the children—and perhaps therein lies the difference.

Equally important, at forty-one I was a very different person than I had been at twenty-four, when I married the first time, or at thirty-one, when I married for the second. My older self looks back at those younger selves with a bemused expression on her face and not just a little, almost maternal sympathy, recognizing that I simply wasn't ready enough or formed enough or healthy enough to make a connection of permanence and value. Yet once again, the failure of those marriages was, in retrospect, necessary for me to learn what I needed to know about myself to make my end of the partnership work. I'm not sure there was any other way I could have learned it, except through the hard, painful lessons the dissolution of a relationship teaches.

In some sense, remarriage is the most hopeful and optimistic of human gestures. The fact that we can sometimes emerge intact and willing to believe again in the possibility of meaningful connection—in intimacy, sharing, and growth—is nothing less than a testament to the resiliency of the human imagination. And that, after pain and unhappiness, we can sometimes actually allow ourselves to be vulnerable once again—to permit ourselves to love, want, and need each other—is more like a hymn to the wonders of spirit than anything else.

This year, Doug and I will celebrate our seventh year of traveling on a shared path and a decade of relationship. If anything, the intervening years between that magical day in Mendocino and now have brought us closer together through the bonds of experience, as we grow together and raise three children in partnership. The road we travel together isn't always smooth but that is in the nature of life and the journey, and both of us are wise and old enough to understand that.

Finally, I was lucky to meet a man who had, in the course of his own journey, acquired self-knowledge and who was secure enough to dream his own dreams and allow me to dream mine. In the end, it is mutual respect and admiration for each other's talents and gifts and the ways in which we are different, combined with mature love, that keep us on the path together, looking toward the future.

I still have the dress and make sure, from time to time, that I fit into it, for reasons that have nothing to do with vanity and everything to do with a moment in time when the road took a lovely, but unpredicted, turn.

The Power
of Love

⁓∞⁓

SOMETIMES, THE ROAD takes us to places where our spirits are challenged in the deepest sense, and where the essence of the gift of life is revealed to us through the threat of its loss.

I found myself at such a place nearly six years ago and, at that intersection, discovered the meaning of hope.

⁓∞⁓

Once again, a holiday party would change the course of my life. Three years after the evening Doug walked through my front door and eight months or so after we married, we threw a small party in early December for a few close friends. There was much to celebrate; it had been a wonderful year and life was very, very good. I wore a stretchy velvet off-the-shoulder pants outfit my friend Connie had designed that made me feel beautiful and sexy. It was a great party, with good food and better champagne. And, after the guests left, with the lights of the bridge and the marina twinkling in the distance through the windows, it became a night of romance.

The discovery, in January, that I was pregnant at the age of forty-two left us both a bit breathless and light-headed. I remember racing to the drugstore and buying the easiest-to-use pregnancy kit because I, the doctor and surgeon, wasn't entirely sure I was calm enough to follow complicated directions! Sitting on the edge of the bathtub, I looked at the blue stripe which confirmed what, in my heart, I already knew. And while I was concerned about how old I was—my age would make this a high-risk pregnancy by definition—nonetheless this felt so right. I had a husband who loved me as I loved him and a marriage that continued to grow in depth and commitment. Our jobs were solid, and our girls would make terrific older sisters. And while we hadn't planned to expand our family, it was a welcome blessing. And then there was something more: This was the first time I would have a child in the context of partnership. This time, there would be someone by my side, to feel the kicks and share in the miracle of life burgeoning within me. This time, I would give birth not alone but with my husband at my side, and this child would begin her life with two loving parents.

For once, the future looked blissfully uncomplicated.

We all settled in to the news. The first ultrasound made it all seem deliciously real, and I sent it off to Doug via fax—he was in Lillehammer, Norway covering alpine skiing in the 1994 Winter Olympics for CBS—with the words "A future downhiller, perhaps?" scribbled in the margin.

It never occurred to me that our child would be anything but a girl. I may have a rather limited imagination but I saw myself, the feminist mother, raising three strong-willed daughters. Kate and Rachel's last name remained Snyderman, so there was the question of which last name to give the new baby. Doug and I agreed, on handshake late at night in bed, that if it was a girl (and, of course, I knew it would be), she would have my last name and, if a boy, he would have Doug's. No problem. When the amniocentesis results came in—I was in Little Rock visiting Connie when I got the page—I did gasp just a little when I learned the baby I was carrying was a boy. (Surprise, surprise! A boy! was my first thought. My second: How *do* you raise a boy? Yikes!) The road had taken another new turn.

Life seemed full of blessings, large and small. The girls were thriving, and my pregnancy was, thankfully, uneventful. I enjoy being pregnant—mercifully, I don't get morning sickness—and actually enjoy the way my body feels, and this time, I wasn't in it alone. I was loved and supported. The months passed and the family's excitement grew as I approached my due date of September first. Kate, in particular, wanted to participate in the birth and asked repeatedly if she could be in the delivery room. I didn't want her there because things can and often do go wrong in delivery, while Doug worried that she would find it hard to see me in pain. Both sets of grandparents thought it was a bad idea. But eight-year-old Kate wouldn't let go—she is both strong-willed and resilient—and finally asked if I would ask the obstetrician. If the doctor said "no," Kate would fold her tents, and I was pretty sure my doctor would be on my side.

To my surprise, my doctor, Laurie Green (who had also delivered Rachel and had known Kate since she was two), thought Kate was emotionally ready and confident enough to take part if she wanted to (she'd already come to a number of my office visits). Moreover, the hospital had a program to include siblings in the birth process. The program took a sensible approach: It made it clear to the child that she could change her mind at any time and leave the room, and required that she have a "coach" of her own to help her. We were swayed by Laurie's arguments—particularly by the value of the bonding experience for Kate—and decided that Angie, my assistant, would be her coach. We planned for Kate to take the class the following Saturday which would prepare her for the physical events of a normal delivery. Then I had a brainstorm of my own: Wouldn't this make a great segment for *Good Morning America*? The story could focus on Kate, the program for siblings, and the idea of including the family in the birth process. It wouldn't be about me at all and I wouldn't even need to be on camera. (Sure, Nancy. How do you do a story about delivery without showing the mother? What was I thinking? The last week of a pregnancy may not be, in the end, a time of great clarity . . .) But *Good Morning America* loved the idea, and I got to pick the producer, the cameraperson, and the sound person.

Rachel, who was almost six, made up her own mind. She decided to stay at home, and just told us to bring her the new baby brother when it was over.

My water broke on Sunday, August 21, which was also Doug's thirty-seventh birthday, and we headed off to the hospital. My labor was easy and short, and the delivery uneventful, if slightly unusual in that it was attended by a rather large group of people and would be seen by over ten million people on national television the following day. (It was on *Good Morning America* in the morning, and then was re-aired on *Oprah*. And in the end, there was more of me on camera than I ever bargained for.) Kate looked and felt terrifically grown-up and proud. She stood at my feet in a surgical gown, adult-sized gloves, and goggles, and was a thoroughly excellent coach ("Mom, you only have three contractions left." "Oh Mom, he's crowning!" "Push, Mom, push. Oh man, his head's so big!"). She watched her brother emerge into the world and actually cut the umbilical cord. Doug sat by my head, holding my hand and talking to me in a low, steady voice; he was an enormous source of strength as we witnessed the birth of our child together.

Charles Brett Myers was a beautiful full-term baby, weighing in at seven pounds, two ounces, and perfectly formed. Doug had gotten the birthday present of a lifetime, and I was tired but profoundly happy.

We called family and friends with our wondrous news and, after a few hours, Angie took Kate home. In the now quiet hospital room, Doug and I sat together, talking and eating some pasta with the contentment that comes of shared experience, while Charlie slept in a bassinet in the corner of the room. By coincidence, the labor nurse, Barb Silver, was the one I'd had when Rachel was born, and it had been good to see a familiar face. She was on that Sunday evening, and I watched as she came in to check on the baby. She hung over him for a few minutes, said nothing, and then left. Moments later, she returned with another nurse. They were soon joined by a third.

As a doctor, I knew immediately that this much attention was not a good thing. Charlie's color remained fine but he was starting to breathe too quickly. The nurses alerted the pediatrician on call.

On the pediatrician's recommendation, Charlie was moved to the Intensive Care Unit as a precaution, but the doctor counseled us not to worry. I held my breath as I heard the word "precaution," knowing, as a doctor, that in a hospital "precautions" are always a cause for worry.

The pediatrician came back with the results of the baby's chest X ray. Instead of clear, black images, his lung fields on the X ray were fluffy and white. This might just be amniotic fluid remaining in his lungs, fluid that did not get squeezed out as he passed through the birth canal. But it could be something much more serious, a life-threatening newborn infection called Group B strep.

Babies can be colonized with strep as they pass through the birth canal, and in a matter of hours, a deadly infection can take hold. I had, as a pediatric resident, dealt with the condition, and knew that the only way to treat it was with aggressive use of intravenous antibiotics. I was also painfully aware that one of the antibiotics was known to cause deafness in some newborns, medical knowledge that only increased my maternal anxiety.

I tried to reassure myself that they would just hold him for forty-eight hours while the antibiotics took effect and that, once the blood cultures came back clean, we would all go home as a family.

Doug went home to Kate and Rachel that night, and I tossed and turned, sleepless. They never brought Charlie back to my room the next morning, Monday, when I was scheduled to be released. Ironically, the *Good Morning America* segment aired that morning, and good wishes and presents poured in from all over the country. By Monday afternoon, it was clear the baby would not be going home anytime soon. My OB-GYN bought me another day in the hospital but on Tuesday I left without a baby in my arms. If anything, Charlie's X ray showed that the condition had worsened.

Slowly, joy gave way, first, to shock and then, later, to fear.

My only son lay in an isolette in the ICU, surrounded by high-tech equipment, monitors, and tubing, IVs in his beautiful little hand and high up on his forehead, near the scalp. There were fourteen or so other isolettes, protecting babies born prematurely or with other problems, most of whom were lying under bilirubin lights to prevent jaundice. He was the only plump, full-term baby in the room. And although I had been a pediatrics resident and knew the role of every bit of equipment attached to his small body—how his tiny hand was tethered to keep him from dislodging the IV and why the little cup was taped to his forehead—nothing, no amount of experience or knowledge, prepared me for how I felt when I saw the child I had just brought into the world lying there.

The severity of an infant's condition was, in part, indicated by the presence or absence of a rocking chair by the isolette's side: I watched as the luckier mothers rocked back and forth, their infants in their arms. There was no rocking chair by Charlie's isolette and the familiar surgical gown I put on to see him took on a special and very painful significance. For nearly twenty years, I'd gowned to protect myself as a doctor and to bring to others whatever measure of the healing arts I possessed. It was the article of clothing which, along with the white coat, made me feel confident and sure of my abilities. Now I wore it to protect my own child from the bacteria

I carried in from the outside world. Like the plastic walls of the isolette, the gown separated me from the child I longed to hold, and inside of the gown, I felt helpless. I unscrewed the porthole on the side of the isolette, and touched him with my hand. Tears rolled down my cheeks as I watched the muscles between his ribs strain with every breath.

And I went home in an emotional limbo that I still can't really put into words. I tried to keep my fears at bay. I pumped my breasts and froze the milk in anticipation of Charlie's homecoming, and Doug and I busied ourselves with projects. The five of us were to move to a new house in a just a month's time and we ran errands—picking out tile, marble, and new bathroom fixtures—as if a happy future with three healthy children would come more quickly if we did. I did my best not to think about or analyze why Charlie was stable but not getting better; I reminded myself that he was in the best hands possible. We drove back and forth to the hospital to see him, touching him lightly through the porthole. Angie, my assistant, kept the world at bay—I couldn't talk to anyone except Doug's parents and mine—and we fussed over Kate and Rachel. We had told them as little as we could about why their brother wasn't home in his crib. What energy I had left I devoted to the children and staying in one piece.

Doug and I were standing side by side in my office at home when the hospital called at 2:30 p.m. on Wednesday afternoon. Charlie was breathing so quickly that the lining of his lung had popped, allowing air from the outside of the lung to get in and depress the lung tissue. The condition is called pneumothorax, and it is a very serious complication which, left untreated, can cause respiratory or heart failure. Treatment is invasive: A needle is stuck into the infant's chest to draw off the excess air. If the procedure fails, the next step is to place a tube into the baby's chest.

I gave my permission and, totally undone, burst into tears. I knew all too well the pattern that complications take on in hospital settings; they rarely resolve themselves easily and often snowball, one complication giving way to another. A dark window opened up in my soul as I allowed myself to realize, for the first time, that my newborn son, a scant three days old, might possibly die.

❦

I felt myself unraveling bit by bit, the stress of Charlie's immediate crisis compounded by a flood of postpartum hormones. I was both numb and rubbed raw with feeling at once. I was torn between begging the medical staff to let me hold my child and fearful that my touching him and taking him out of the isolette, his protective shield, would put him at greater risk. I was desperate to touch him yet found myself braced against the terrible, impossible thought that I might lose him. Doug stayed calmer on the outside than I—I was bent double like a palm tree in gale-force winds, tearful and weepy—though inside, he grew angrier, railing at the unfairness of life, hating the hospital, wanting to hold on to the normalcy of early Sunday. The fast reversals—from the unmitigated joy of early Sunday afternoon to where we found ourselves, first on Sunday evening and then on Wednesday—were too much for both of us. Each of us reacted to the crisis at hand in different ways and, in doing so, we began to be of little help to the other. I talked a blue streak about superficial details, but inside I was holing up. I became uncommunicative about all that really mattered, more out of superstition than anything else; putting what was possible into words made it real. If I didn't talk about it, then the worst couldn't, wouldn't happen.

But then, at the same time, I was also the mother of two girls. As a physician *and* a mother, I felt they needed to see their baby brother and to acknowledge his existence, not just because he was late in coming home but because he might *never* sleep in the room we had planned for him. I thought seeing him was equally critical for both girls: Kate, after all, had literally helped bring him into the world, while Rachel had never seen him. Doug was adamantly opposed to my plan to bring the girls to the hospital and into the ICU. He thought the experience would be too much for the girls, that they were too young to handle the tubes, the wires, the bells, the monitors, and everything else that is frightening about an Intensive Care Unit. He was speaking from the heart, and I realized how very different his experience of the hospital had been from mine. If my medical expertise opened me to expecting the worse, at least the setting didn't frighten me. I realized that we were afraid of different things. But at the same time, I was convinced that some kind of closure was terribly important to the girls and to all of us as a family. I prevailed but I had only convinced Doug on the surface.

The girls drew pictures for the baby with the words "I love you" written in crayon, and brought him a Peter Rabbit toy and a teddy bear. We all went to the hospital on Thursday afternoon, and into the ICU. The girls put on gowns, washed their hands, and walked to the isolette in which their brother lay. Their faces lit up—Rachel was seeing him for the first time and Kate clearly knew how worried we were—and I felt a wave of gladness wash over me. They put their hands into the isolette, and touched him.

And at that moment, all of Charlie's monitors

went off. Excited by the girls' presence, his heart rate and breathing had been dangerously accelerated.

❧

The nurses ushered us out of the ICU quickly and firmly. I saw the confusion etched on the girls' faces give way first to dismay and then to tears. Doug stood there glaring, furious. I turned to face him. "I told you this was a bad idea," he shouted at me, his finger pointing, and his loud voice echoing through the hospital halls. His face stricken and angry at once, it was clear he thought we had risked Charlie's recovery. He stormed out, and I ran after him, to no avail. Walking back, I tried to calm myself down. I took the girls to the waiting room, and went back into the ICU alone, and stood by Charlie's isolette, watching the nurses rearrange the monitors, feeling devastated and utterly helpless. One of the nurses pulled me aside and suggested that I tell my husband to come back alone. I told her that I was sure he wouldn't; for one thing, he was too angry and, for another, he honestly believed that we were harming, not helping, Charlie by our presence. She pressed me to try anyway, suggesting that I tell him it was "nurse's orders." The three of us drove home alone; I had no idea where Doug had gone.

Doug had walked off most of his anger by the time he got home but, as I expected, he had no intention of going back to the hospital. I pleaded with him, saying the nurse had insisted that he come back alone, and finally, he relented. He left home around five p.m.

I got the kids dinner and into bed, and waited for him with the television blaring to make the house seem less empty. The telephone never rang. Hours passed and, finally, at eleven p.m., now worried about both my son and my husband, I called the ICU and asked for the nurse.

What she had to tell me was nothing less than miraculous. Doug had gone back into the ICU, hesitant and concerned that his presence might again excite the baby. The nurse reassured him and had him stand there, his hand inside the isolette. He stood there for a long time, thinking, watching his son. After a time, the nurse brought over a rocking chair, took Charlie out of the isolette—still attached to the monitor wires and IV tubing—and put him in Doug's arms.

They rocked together for hours, father and son, in the quiet of the ICU, and the nurses gave them a wide berth. By the time I called late that night, Charlie's breathing had slowed and his heart rate was normal. By the following morning, Friday, his chest X ray was clear, and I was able to nurse him for the first time. There are no words to describe what I felt when he was returned to my arms. I asked, and the doctors agreed, that he be taken off antibiotics.

And on Monday morning, we took Charlie home.

Looking at him now, a rambunctious and irrepressible five-going-on-six-year-old, it's hard for me to imagine that he was ever as desperately sick as he was, or that we came so close to losing him.

But I make a point of remembering.

꿍

My mother put it simply and wisely: "Never underestimate the power of love." There is no question in my mind about what happened that Thursday night in the ICU. Our son was healed by his father's love, brought to wellness by his father's touch. Antibiotics alone could not—and did not—bring Charlie back from the brink; it was, I honestly believe, a combination of modern science and the power of love.

That difficult week taught myriad lessons. I recognized that Doug had been able to do something for our child that I could not, and I learned a special respect for that bond between father and son. I had, somehow, in the course of the week, without really knowing it, given up no small measure of hope and, in giving up hope, I was unable to access the most important resource I had in getting me through the crisis: spirit. I'm not entirely sure why it happened—perhaps it was nothing more complicated than my medical knowledge crowding out my sense of possibility—but I know that Doug's energy was fueled by hope and mine was not. While I prepared for the bleakest of outcomes, Doug's hopefulness allowed him to scan the horizon for light.

And his hope, his spirit, his love saved our child's life.

The simplicity of the word "hope" belies the importance hope plays in human life. Hope lets us look to the future, even when the moment we are living is hard and painful. Hope rallies our strengths, our natural defenses, at those times when we are most besieged. And, finally, in times of sickness, hope—whether it finds its expression in faith or religious belief or simply in positive expectations—is our best ally, as the pioneering work of both Dr. Herbert Benson in his book *The Mind/Body Effect*, and, more popularly, Dr. Bernie Siegel has made abundantly clear. Mind and body, in both health and sickness, are parts of a single whole.

As a physician, I relearned in more personal terms what I had known intellectually: the important role of spirit or hopefulness in healing the body. As we approach the new millennium, modern medicine has finally come to acknowledge and explore the profound connections between body and spirit, and as patients, we have every right to insist that our physicians and health care providers see us as whole.

And we must remind ourselves, no matter where the road takes us, to hold on to hope. The poet Emily Dickinson, perhaps, said it best:

> "Hope" is the thing with feathers—
> That perches in the soul—
> And sings the tune without the words—
> And never stops—at all—
>
> And sweetest—in the Gale—is heard—
> And sore must be the storm—
> That could abash the little Bird
> That kept so many warm—
>
> I've heard it in the chillest land—
> And on the strangest Sea—
> Yet, never, in Extremity,
> It asked a crumb—of Me.

Navigating
by the Stars

∞

I LOOK BACK at my girlhood self, dreaming her dreams in her room in Fort Wayne, Indiana, and I realize that it's not simply the journey—the getting here—that is different from what I imagined, nor is it where I've ended up: with a second career in television that has connected me to the larger world in ways I never thought possible. Lying on my bed, all those years ago, I never imagined the continuing challenges and conflicts my own choices—deciding both to have a career and to be a mother—would engender. I chose this path comparatively late, at the age of thirty-four, but there's rarely a day when I'm not keenly aware that I don't have a map or guidebook to show me how to do it right, or even a compass to tell me I'm on the right track. Most of the time, I feel as though I'm out on the waters by myself, navigating by the stars alone, and, sometimes, not doing it as well as I should or as others might.

Do we all, I wonder, sit alone in our kitchens, after the children are asleep, imagining that every other woman in America is managing far better than we are?

Reconciling our own needs with the needs of those we love—particularly the children we have brought into the world and covenanted to raise—sometimes seems painfully, impossibly out of reach.

Images of the "perfect" mother haunt each and every one of us, whether we choose to stay at home with our children or try to combine motherhood with work and career. (It's worth noting that while the "perfect" mother is, by traditional definition, a stay-at-home mom, in her book *The Myths of Motherhood*, Shari Thurer points out that fewer than 7 percent of American families are made up of breadwinner fathers and homemaker mothers. The truth is that, for the majority of women, staying at home is not an economically viable choice, even if they want to.)

The "perfect" mother hasn't changed much since the 1950s of my childhood when, in black and white, she was beamed into American living rooms on *Ozzie and Harriet* and *Father Knows Best*. She is always available, always empathetic, always nurturing, and eternally sunny. She is never tired or angry or frustrated. She is, for all intents and purposes, a woman without a self, without personal ambition, yet she manages to possess a singular kind of wisdom. She knows precisely how to nurture without smothering, how to find the balance between structure and independence. She is just, in the way that only the truly selfless are, and incapable of a temper tantrum of her own. She never makes mistakes or disappoints and so, lucky woman, she will never be the object of her child's anger or the subject of her child's therapy.

That the perfect mother doesn't really exist except as a cultural icon doesn't prevent her from making many women, myself included, abjectly self-critical and unhappy from time to time. Her perfectly shaped homemade cookies, her endless patience, and her unflappable disposition comprise the impossible, mythical standard against which we end up measuring ourselves. Worse still, because she dominates the cultural mythology of motherhood, we find ourselves, as women and mothers, navigating by the stars, making it up as we go along.

And at times, it isn't easy. And it's definitely harder than it needs to be.

∽

Spring brought our first family vacation to Europe, and the children, particularly Kate and Rachel, were really looking forward to it. We'd rented a London flat, rather than staying in a hotel, which we thought would be easier on all three children, but especially almost-five-year-old Charlie. There's so much to see in London, and I thought it the perfect place for the children's first exposure to a different culture. We'd just come in from our first excursion, a glorious morning under amazingly sunny skies at the London Horse and Harness Parade (the girls, like their mother, are avid riders and compete themselves), when the urgent message came in from ABC News in New York. The news of the crisis in Kosovo had just broken. Doug immediately said, "I bet they want you in Albania," but I answered, "No way. They know I'm on vacation."

I called in and, indeed, the producers of *Good Morning America*, and *20/20* were sure that the refugee story would quickly become a medical story, because cholera and other communicable diseases thrive in overcrowded and unsanitary conditions. How soon could I go? I told them I had to talk to my family, and promised I'd call back in an hour. Even before I'd hung up, I already knew what I wanted to do and, thank goodness, without missing a beat, Doug looked at me and said, "This is your job. You have to go." He was perfectly okay about staying in London alone with the children until I returned. Minutes later, I was back on the telephone to New York, and arrangements had been made for me to fly the next day to Thessaloniki in Greece and then be driven almost four hours through the mountains toward the border of Macedonia and Kosovo. Hearing my news, the children were clearly very disappointed.

The next morning, my daughters were more subdued than I would have liked. We went off to the Tower of London to gawk at the Crown Jewels and hear the story of the young princes, and then had lunch at an English pub, a lunch I knew I would have to leave before we had even finished eating. I felt terrible and conflicted about leaving my family, particularly when Rachel asked, for what must have been the tenth time, "Don't the people at ABC know we're on vacation, Mommy?" But, at the same time, I didn't really have the courage to simply say I was going because I wanted to, because it was important to me to witness these events firsthand. The myth of the perfect mother is hard to shake off, even when you are thousands of miles away from your own kitchen. I told a partial truth: "It's Mommy's job." That isn't untrue: Reporting is my job and, like any other woman or man who has one boss or several, I try hard not to disappoint mine. But there was, of course, more: The conflict between the self and mother isn't, I think, ever easy. On the one hand, I knew perfectly well that, if I'd said no, ABC would have either sent someone else or had one of the correspondents on hand give the report I might have given. On the other, I didn't want to say "no."

∞

The memory is so vivid that I need to tell it as if it happened only today.

I arrive at London's Heathrow Airport with a heavy heart but I don't turn back. I board my plane along with some of the crew from the ABC London bureau, happy to have the company. At midnight, I find myself in a car speeding through the mountains toward the Macedonian border, feeling more than just a little on edge. Passing through the border patrol is less than pleasant—the officials there seem committed to making it as time-consuming and difficult a passage as possible—but we make it through without mishap. ABC has managed to find a little hotel still partly under construction for us to stay in; the rooms are bare and there is no service but it's better than sleeping in the camps in a sleeping bag, the only other alternative.

After just a few hours' sleep, we go to Blace, a refugee camp on the bank of a river, just across the border from Kosovo. I am not a war correspondent and the landscape is, to my eyes, more than a little surreal: High in a tower, the blue-uniformed Macedonian guards stand watch, machine guns in their hands, as the beams of the searchlights scan the train tracks and hills that lead up to the mountains of Kosovo for human movement.

I am unprepared for what we discover. The air smells of sewage, damp, mud, and rotting food. Instead of a camp teeming with humanity, we find a place of hurried abandonment: piles of refuse, discarded tents and blankets, and dozens and dozens of personal items littering the ground, testifying to the disorderly exodus of thousands of people. I pick up a black-and-white photograph of a young woman sunbathing on a raft in the middle of a lake, a memento of happier times hurriedly dropped. I see a pair of baby shoes and a stroller, a baby's bottle, eyeglasses half-submerged in a puddle. There are all manner of belongings languishing in the muddy field.

It is not geography alone that separates me from London and my family.

The story, as we and the world are soon to discover, was that thousands of people were forcibly evacuated by the Macedonian police, gun butts at their backs, the men separated from the women and children and, in many cases, the children separated from their mothers. The refugees have been moved to two NATO camps, one run by the French and the other by the British, and we go to the British camp next. There I meet doctors, bankers, computer experts, college professors, and musicians, and not a single family that is intact. I meet a ten-year-old boy who was shot in the back while trying to escape soldiers. They left him for dead in the woods. I talk to a thirteen-year-old girl, Lindita—the same age as my daughter Kate, with the same prepubescent body— who, separated from her parents, has spent the night sleeping in a tent with nine or ten strangers. Overnight, she has had to learn to fend for herself. Her eyes, empty and tearless, are ringed with signs of sleeplessness.

It is impossible for me to react dispassionately. I see the child before me and I try to conceive of her mother's pain and fear in the wake of this terrible separation, but they are beyond my imagining. How can she bear the thoughts that must be going through her mind? How can she survive not knowing if her daughter is safe? Can she find the words to pray? I look around the field and envision the women and children huddled within wet blankets and the terrible futility of trying to comfort a cold, tired, and hungry youngster in these circumstances. I feel surrounded by the sound of children's tears.

A woman approaches us, saying that there isn't enough food in the camp, and that her children are hungry. We hand her our bananas and sandwiches and, as she thanks us, her eyes well up.

By comparison, remembering the mundane, if sometimes exhausting, details of life with my own children makes me feel small and petty. I see myself snapping when a nap-deprived Charlie whines during an afternoon of boring but necessary errands. The girls bickering in the kitchen after I've spent a long day seeing patients, when I want nothing more than some time alone, tending to no one. My irritation when, at the last minute, one of my daughters comes home with a long-term assignment that she's been carrying around in her backpack for days on end and which, she tells me, is due tomorrow.

I suddenly, desperately, miss my children. I know that, unlike the children in the tents, mine are safe and dry, but that doesn't stop me from longing for them. I can't call them—I've only been able to get word to them that I'm fine—and I miss hearing their voices and, even more, their laughter, in a place where there is none.

That night, when the crew repairs to the hotel, Charlie Gibson asks me why I have come on this trip. Coming from a friend of long standing, the father of two girls of his own, his question unnerves me. After all, he reminds me, I had every right to say that my obligations to my family came first. I find myself telling him I really didn't want to come but thought that I had to, because it was my job.

I haven't been entirely straight with my children and, now, I waffle with a good friend and colleague. But I leave it at that, and don't allow myself to elaborate. Instead, I go to a bar with a few colleagues and, deep in my heart, curse the perfect mother, whoever and wherever she is.

I am physically tired and emotionally exhausted by all I have seen and all that I am feeling, but I'm too keyed up to sleep. I end up taking a sleeping pill, and wake up feeling more human than I have since the telephone rang in London. We do our second live broadcast from the British-run NATO camp and, during the break, I tell Charlie I have something to tell him after the show. The show is solid, a series of interviews with people who have been thrown together, their lives precipitously linked by events and history, twelve strangers desperately trying to function as a unit, almost as a family does. It escapes no one that these are all people who have lost their intimate connections to the past, perhaps permanently, and that there seems to be no future.

The broadcast over, I turn to Charlie Gibson, and

tell him the unvarnished truth: that while I didn't want to leave Doug and the children, I wanted and needed to cover the story. Without intending to, I burst into tears, feeling as guilty and crummy about myself as a mother as I ever have. Every ambivalence I have ever felt about the choices I've made in my life seems to rise suddenly to the surface and with the perspective of the refugee camps vivid in my mind—the misery and suffering of parents and children alike—I feel ashamed and unworthy of my children's love.

Why is it that I feel so diminished and conflicted when a part of me knows full well that the experience of being in Kosovo was important? That the experience has changed me in ways that matter, both as a mother and a woman? When I have done some of the best reporting of my life?

Why do I feel this way even though I know there will be other opportunities for me to share London with the kids and that, besides, they've had a wonderful time with Doug?

The shadow of the perfect mother looms large.

∞

The work done, we drove through the mountains in the middle of the night to get to Greece, so that I could catch a flight to London to rejoin the family on Saturday, in time to fly back to San Francisco on Sunday. I had been gone six days. I left Athens in the morning and made it back to London by noon. The flat was empty—Doug and the children were off somewhere—and I took a much needed shower. The water running off of my body was actually brackish and brown, a reminder that a part of Kosovo was still with me. I wiped down the mud-splattered clogs I wore both in the camps and back on the plane. There was a note from Doug that he'd made a reservation for me and the girls to have high tea at the Ritz—a posh way to experience an English ritual—and that they were really looking forward to it. I got dressed in a black skirt and sweater and pearls (the Ritz doesn't allow women in pants, and informal clothes are discreetly, but firmly, discouraged) and waited for the family to get back.

The reunion with my family was all I could have hoped for, and the girls and I headed for the Ritz, first taking the underground—the London subway—and then walking from the green of Hyde Park to the Ritz, at the corner of St. James's and Piccadilly. The Ritz is in one of the most elegant parts of London, just steps away from the beautiful and expensive shops on Bond Street and within walking distance of the royal palaces. We were ushered into a beautiful, high-ceilinged room, complete with gilded moldings and potted palms. It is a place of quiet elegance: exquisite china and porcelain, bouquets of flowers, and well-dressed patrons. The girls are animated but act very grown-up, inspired by the surroundings and the pretty dresses they have on. High tea was delicious and sumptuous: tiny sandwiches, followed by scones, clotted cream, lemon curd, and of course, tea served in delicate cups.

I felt tremendously dislocated, as if I'd entered some sort of parallel universe by accident. How could tea at the Ritz coexist on a single planet, much less a single continent, with the camps I'd just left? It was as though I hadn't traveled far enough to make the transition. How could I find myself in a such an orderly, elegant world—a place that gave no hint of the shattered and broken lives I'd just witnessed firsthand—after only a short plane ride?

It was my two daughters who helped me bridge the gap between the two worlds of London and the refugee camps, and the roles of mother and correspondent. They asked me question after question, particularly about what had happened to the children in the camps. Their interest was genuine, different from the usual "Okay, Mom, we've heard enough" reaction I feared I would hear. As we talked, I saw that the enormous complexity of the world they lived in began to become real through my stories. I took a deep breath, reveling in the moment, and felt enormously proud of both of them.

And, for just a brief moment, I saw myself as they saw me, and I held my head high.

∞

I realize, as I write this, that even my own mother, who, in my eyes at least, was a wonderful and loving parent, also suffered by comparison with the cultural icon we call the perfect mother. True to the spirit of the 1950s, my mother gave up a career of her own in art to become a wife and homemaker, raising four children and running a household of six with flexibility, humor, and grace. I can't even begin to tally how many scout meetings she must have gone to over the years, how many cookies she must have baked, or how many homework assignments she must have corrected.

But she didn't see herself as perfect because she, too, lived in the shadow of the myth of total selflessness. And for all the enormous sacrifices my mother made for her family, she still had a strong sense of self. When I was about ten and my mother thirty-four, she suddenly announced she was going off to Martha's Vineyard with some old friends from art school. Looking back as an adult, I think she was probably just exhausted by the endless need to be perfect at everything she did. Now mind you, this was 1963 in Fort Wayne, Indiana; think hats and white gloves for church on Sundays and remember that, by the standards of the day, a woman who worked was married to a man who couldn't take care of her. Mothers of four didn't, of an evening, suddenly stand up and announce that they were going off by themselves when there were lunches to be packed, laundry to be done. (Did Harriet ever take a weekend off? How would Ozzie have coped?) My father did pretty much what most of his golfing buddies would have done in his shoes: He looked up and said she wasn't going. And she answered by saying that, yes, she was. It was all organized: She'd arranged for someone to watch us, and the refrigerator was stocked with meals, ready to be warmed up. My father repeated himself and, again, my mother answered.

As I remember it, no one ever shouted. It was a calm, decisive battle, a test of wills, with two adults volleying back and forth: "Yes, I am." "No, you're not." I kept hearing the words "Martha's Vineyard" and, since my sister's name is Martha, I didn't understand what her vineyard was or what it had to do with my parents' argument.

I guess my father must have thought he had the

problem solved because, when he left for work the next morning, he reminded my mother that he expected her in the usual place—home, that is—when he got back. But when he did get home, she was—astonishingly enough—gone.

Never to be outdone, my father decided to give my mother a homecoming she'd never forget. He took us to the local drugstore, bought posterboard, and organized what may have been the Fort Wayne airport's first demonstration. In 1963 there wasn't any airport security, and when my mother's plane came to a stop, the first thing she saw on the tarmac was her husband accompanied by her four children, each of whom carried a hand-lettered sign. I still remember what mine said, in big, black, wobbly letters: MOMMY, MOMMY, WHY DID YOU LEAVE US? The whole episode testifies to the quirky sense of humor that has kept my parents in sync with each other for nearly fifty years.

My mother walked toward us laughing, a spring in her step. She looked younger and happier than she had in a while, after just three days of tending to herself and no one else.

I know now what I didn't know then, standing on the tarmac, holding my sign. My mother had, by doing something for herself alone, renewed her spirit. She'd beaten back the shadow cast by the perfect mother and, by doing so, gave herself and her children a great gift.

And by holding on to her own sense of self throughout the years, she has always given her eldest daughter permission to follow her own dreams.

∞

Every woman I know who is a mother struggles with the legacy of the perfect mother. Hardest of all to manage, I think, is the theme of self-sacrifice that animates the myth because if, as the myth tells us, self-sacrifice is the keystone of perfect mothering, then its obverse, choosing for ourselves, is a mark of the clearly imperfect mother. That, of course, lies at the heart of everything I felt about going to Kosovo, and even writing about it. I actually wondered out loud if telling the story made me sound selfish. It is the reason Leslie automatically feels guilty if she finds herself looking foward to three hours alone when her seven-year-old daughter goes off on a playdate. It is why Mary Ellen, after a long day at the office, rushes home to her children, even though sometimes what she'd really like to do is spend time just window-shopping, decompressing from the day, or meeting a friend for drinks. Anything over the nine hours she's already spent making a living outside of her children's world makes her feel self-indulgent and selfish. Liza, a former publishing executive, confides that, for years, the only times she ever felt totally unconflicted about the balancing act of motherhood and work was in transit between the office and home. With wit, she describes it as the "Zen of traveling," that moment between places when you can actually imagine you are doing both things well and that you're not making the wrong choice.

But on reflection, I wonder if the total self-sacrifice the myth demands is a good thing—either for our children or for us. Why would a woman who always puts herself last be a good model for anyone, much less her sons and daughters? Dr. Carin Rubenstein, in her book *The Sacrificial Mother*, puts it in proper perspective: "To be able to care for others well, a woman needs to learn to be able to love herself. To give to others, she has to learn to take for herself. If mothers could show themselves only a fraction of the affection and attention they give their children, they'd be so much better off. They need to reserve some emotional energy for themselves, make some room for their own needs and desires and dreams."

It isn't that a certain amount of self-sacrifice isn't a part of motherhood. Of course it is, because caretaking requires that, at times, we put the needs of others first. But there is a point of balance, and a woman's complete self-sacrifice shouldn't and cannot be a condition of successful parenting. We need, in the circle of women, to sit down together and realize that the myth of the perfect mother is just that: a myth. And that we need, as we approach the millennium, a new, more productive mythology of motherhood, one that nurtures our spirits as we nurture our children. As Shari Thurer puts it in *The Myths of Motherhood*, "When mothers are able to see through the mythology, they may see that their 'failures' stem not necessarily from personal defects, but from the way society is structured. When mothers understand the biases inherent in our current conception of good mothering, they may learn to select among the rules and begin to create their own philosophy of child rearing, one that works for themselves and their children."

We need to stop equating caring for ourselves with neglect or lack of love. We have to help each other find solutions to the problem of balancing all that we need and want to do by insisting that, as a society, we recognize the needs of both children and women through the creation of child-care agencies and programs. We need to make it easier to sail our boats beneath the stars.

Forty-five years ago, Anne Morrow Lindbergh, writer and diarist, the wife of Charles Lindbergh and the mother of five, wrote *Gift from the Sea*, an extraordinary book about balance in women's lives that ought to be required reading for every woman and girl, man and boy. I'd like to close with her words, not simply because they are so wonderfully written but because, even now, on the cusp of a new millennium, they are so true and wise:

> For to be a woman is to have interests and duties, raying out in all directions from the central mother-core, like spokes from the hub of a wheel. The pattern of our lives is essentially circular. We must be open to all points of the compass; husband, children, friends, home, community; stretched out, exposed, sensitive like a spider's web to each breeze that blows, to each call that comes. How difficult for us, then, to achieve a balance in the midst of these contradictory tensions, and yet how necessary for the proper functioning of our lives. . . . The problem is not merely one of *Woman and Career*, *Woman and the Home*, *Woman and Independence*. It is more basically: how to remain whole in the midst of the distractions of life; how to remain balanced, no matter what centrifugal forces tend to pull one off center; how to remain strong, no matter what shocks come in at the periphery and tend to crack the hub of the wheel.

These are words to remember, especially late at night, when the children are asleep and we find ourselves in our kitchens, all alone.

Moon Magic

❧

IT IS LATE in the evening and early autumn in Northern California. I am in the backyard, taking time alone. The breezes still carry a hint of the summer just past and the drying leaves, almost ready to turn, rustle softly. Above me, the full moon hangs in the sky like a giant pearl, illuminating small details in the shadowy landscape. In the moonlight, ordinary things—the contours of a path, the outlines of the tall pampas grass, the fringed edge of a flower—take on aspects of mystery invisible to the eye at noon. It feels as though, bathed in the moonlight, a part of me comes out of the shadows, newly revealed.

In the moonlight, knowledge takes a different form. The wisdom of the noontime sun is sharply analytical. It is the light of cold reason, of differentiation and contrast. The surgeon in me is sunlit. In contrast, the wisdom of the moon is that of meaningful interconnection and relationship, of nuance and subtlety. In the moonlight, first and foremost, I am woman, mother, wife.

At this point in my life, as I approach my forty-eighth year, the moon takes on a special meaning. It is no accident that, since ancient times, the moon has always and universally been seen as feminine in nature. The cycles of the moon so closely echo the cycle of a woman's body—the walls of the uterus waxing and waning in the same rhythm as that of the celestial body in the sky, each beginning anew roughly every twenty-eight days—that even our language records the relationship. "Moon," "month," "menstruation," and "measure" are all cognate words because human beings first told time by the moon's cycles.

For thousands of years, women were thought to possess a special wisdom and power precisely because of the moon magic of their bodies. They alone of the species could bleed without dying; only they could give birth.

The mystery of birth—the bloodless month that presaged the swollen body and then the birth and, with it, the return of blood—was echoed in the night sky as the moon was born, grew full and round, died, and then was reborn again. The moon and fecundity were so connected that, for thousands of years, human beings assumed that plants grew by its light, not that of the sun.

Even now, the moon-cycles of our women's bodies hint at the deep connection between our individual selves and the larger workings of nature. Is it possible that once, in history, women actually cycled with the moon, the metaphoric connection made literal? We do not know, of course, but it is worth noting that ancient writings, among them those of Aristotle, accepted it as fact. What we do know is that, in ancient times and now, women together—working or living in close proximity—cycle together. (During religious festivals devoted to moon worship, where women gathered together outside the presence of men, it seems likely that the rhythms of their bodies would have synchronized and then, perhaps, coincided with the rhythm in the sky.) The fact of our cycling together connects us as well to the larger, if unseen, pattern of nature. What makes it happen is the release of pheromones, chemical substances produced in our bodies, which communicate and connect on a level that does not involve our awareness. Pheromones govern the behavior of most of the animal kingdom and we humans are part of it. We are attracted to our mates by pheromone scents without even knowing it, just as we form a moon circle of women, without thinking, the synchronicity of our bodies the physical proof of other ties.

The moon symbolizes both change and continuity, one phase giving way to the next, but always in an eternal pattern of repetition. It is the moon that gives rise to the twice-daily ebb and flow of tides as well as the rippling of the earth's very surface. My body is almost entirely ocean—we are all 98 percent water—and I would swear, sitting here in the moonlight, that I feel the tides within me, connecting me to the larger pattern of sea changes.

If we listen to them, our women's bodies have much to teach us about life and the process of living. Our female bodies, like the tides, teach a lesson of continuous change. The shoreline of the Northern California coast where I live is dotted with tide pools, pockets among outcroppings of rock where the ocean, flowing in, deposits all manner of life. At low tide, crabs scuttle across the wet sand and limpets cling to the rocks, as do sponges, sea anemones, and the occasional sea star. The tide washes in shiny, silvery fish which, when it recedes, retreat to the waters once again. The inner landscape of the tide pool is ever fluid; sometimes, it is a host to life and, at others, it offers but a place of shelter and nourishment, away from the pounding waves.

But the tide pool, like the female body, is itself subject to greater change. The tide pool itself is reshaped by wind, water, weather, and time. It may be absorbed into the land or into the waters; like everything else on the planet, the tide pool has a beginning and an ending. The tide pool, like a woman's body, teaches that the only permanence is impermanence.

In my body, an important pattern that has governed my woman's life—the monthly bleeding that which, at different times, has signaled different things—has begun to change. In my teenage years, the onset of the cycle signaled a new pathway into the unfamiliar territory of young womanhood, a place of change and self-evaluation quite separate from my childhood world. In my twenties, the years of medical school and residency, the cycles of my body marked little more than the passage of calendrical time. Unlike so many other women for whom their twenties mark their passage into motherhood, for me the bleeding simply meant that life had stayed uncomplicated, focused on the self alone for yet another month. In my thirties and forties, my period—or the absence of it —brought a different kind of self-awareness. My fertility, which had never been part of how I defined myself, became part of my inner core. My children, I found, reconnected me to the generations of women before me, all of whom bled by the light of the moon.

Now, my body will begin, slowly, to adjust to a new and unfamiliar rhythm which, for the first time in nearly three decades, will no longer mark time by bleeding or presage, by the absence of blood, the possibility that is new life. The passage is made more poignant and meaningful by my daughters, in whom the cycles of the moon will soon begin, just as mine begin to end. Partly because of my girls—their beginning and then continuing on that part of a woman's journey which I will soon leave— I arrive at this new intersection not with a sense of regret or mourning but with a new understanding of change and process.

Guiding them through the first major passage in their lives, from childhood to adolescence, reminds me of my own passage, all those years ago. I look at Kate and I well remember what it felt to shed an old self and take on another, one that felt vulnerable in the sight of the world, as my body and my thoughts took on new shape. I can still summon up, as I suppose most women can, the discomfort of those years and the effort it took to shrug off the chrysalis of adolescence and find my adult wings. Change is always difficult, and it strikes me that these two passages—the one into the moon cycles and the one out of them—have much more in common than we might think. Leaving behind the now familiar rhythms of the bodies we have lived in so many decades is, for many of us, difficult because we have forgotten how long it took for us to get comfortable with what was then a new self. On reflection, this moment of passage has much in common with that moment in time when, lying on our girlhood beds, we were thrown into turmoil by the thought of leaving the safety of our childhood bodies and selves behind.

Except for one thing: The culture we live in emphasizes not what we might gain from this passage but what we, as women, have lost by going through it. In a word: fertility.

But the passage into another stage of life which menopause signals—the "moon pause" comes at the very end—was, in the master plan of creation, more in the nature of a gift. Given the tremendous risk to survival that childbearing represented until very recently in human history, menopause was most likely a signal that the woman's work necessary to the survival of the species—bearing children—was done. There's no evidence that this was anything but a natural passage, one that actually took a woman's life to a stage of greater safety, and it is no accident, I think, that those who made it safely through the years of peril were honored as wise women, healers, and prophesiers.

But seen through the cultural prism based on the

male model, so different from our own, the mythology of menopause has been no kinder than that of menstruation. (In the parlance of my adolescence, it was "the curse." When my father was in medical school, menstruation was actually described as the "weeping of the uterus." No kidding.) The processes that make our female bodies so different are all about changes that, seen from the vantage point of a male model, are understood as "erratic" or "unreliable," and have created a mythology of the feminine that is, at best, disparaging. Even our language betrays the distrust with which our culture has regarded the female body for the last several thousand years. "Lunacy" was marked by the changes in the moon, and it isn't hard to figure out whether this was most easily applied to women or men, or what the physical cause of "lunacy" was thought to be. The same goes for "hysteria," which was thought to emanate from the uterus (*hyster* means "womb" in Latin). The fate that befell the word "gossip," as Marina Warner has noted in her book *From the Beast to the Blonde*, was similar. "Gossip" began, around the twelfth century, as a unisex word that denoted a godmother or godfather, or one who was present at a christening. A few centuries later, it applied only to female friends who were invited to attend a birth or christening at the mother's bedside. Once it became an all-female group—a circle of women—

it was no time at all until "gossip" came to mean what it does today.

And then there were the words "hag" and "crone," which meaningfully blurred the line between what a woman's old age looked like and what it represented.

Even now, in medical terms, menopause is defined as "ovarian failure."

It's no wonder that, for centuries, menopause was a woman's passage kept under wraps, never discussed or mentioned.

As long as fertility and youth define a woman's role and worth, menopause will remain, from a cultural point of view, a passage to nowhere.

∽

In the last few decades, the passage of menopause, to borrow from the writer Gail Sheehy, is no longer a "silent" one. Books, magazine articles, television segments and shows, and the frank dialogue that accompanies public interest—not to mention the demographics of an aging baby boomer population—have dragged it into the open.

But taking it out into the open is one thing, and giving it a different cultural context is quite another, and much, much harder. Precisely because menopause happens only to women, it throws the part of self that is connected to our individual definition of womanhood into high relief. How we define ourselves as women will affect not only how we navigate the passage but also what we are able to take away from it and make our own.

While each experience of menopause will be different (not even the physical experience can be generalized), the one universal is this: It is a moment when nature takes us by the shoulders and shakes us into awareness. It is a moment when we are literally required to take the passage of time into account. If we have allowed ourselves to be dulled to the cycles of life, if we have permitted ourselves to be swept along unthinking, if we have stopped paying attention to the growth of self, the moon pause will change all that. And as a result, it is less a place of endings than of the interconnection between "then," "now," and "tomorrow." It is an intersection that, by its nature, allows us to look back at where we have been and forward to where we can go with new perspective. It is a place where, should we choose to, we can give the decisions we have made in our lives a meaningful context.

It is a place of letting go and holding on, and learning to know the difference between the things we need to let go of and those we need to keep.

To experience the meaningfulness that the passage

can teach us, we need first to let go of what society teaches us: that this is only a place of loss and lost opportunities. I see my women friends second-guess the living they have done—regretting the children they did not have then and now will never have—without counting, at the same time, the gifts and the freedoms those choices have given them. But holding on to what we have gained by choosing is every bit as as important as acknowledging that every choice has a cost.

We need to let go of what the culture teaches us about age and beauty in a woman. The physical signs of aging that accompany this passage—everything from hair loss to hot flashes—are, in a culture that prizes beauty and youth above all, among the hardest for most of us to bear. But at the same time, can't we help each other to see that there's liberation in all of this too—that we can finally shake off the specter of the prom queen and the supermodel—and find our beauty in different places? We can use this passage to redefine our expectations of our bodies and our understanding of our womanhood. We can set an example for younger women by reminding them that not all of what makes us women is tied to our ovaries or to smooth skin and thick hair. We can use the wisdom and confidence we have gleaned from the journey to remind those younger than we that this is just one passage among many.

We can use this time of our lives to see the larger patterns of life at work, of the cycle of things. Menopause is an event we can only date in retrospect—one year after the last time we have bled—and it forces us to pay attention to the relationship of the present to the future. The passage locates us in time, real time, and that is *not* a bad thing. It tells us that the time to dream our dreams is now, not tomorrow, and to act on them. It tells us that we need to reflect on where we have been and where we want to go.

It is also a time to take charge and to question the venues open to each and every one of us. There is much about menopause that, from a medical point of view, remains mysterious. No one knows the provenance of the hot flash, or even why some women have them and others don't. No one knows why the mental loopiness and forgetfulness—the endless search for car keys—happens. The various alternatives posed by medicine to managing menopause—the use of hormones, for example—require each of us to take our health into our hands, and make our own, informed choices. We need, in every sense of the word, to take *care* of ourselves, and to come to understand this passage as a place of opportunity, not limitation.

Each morning that I am home, I ride a horse, and I ride hard. My horse, Meg, is a beautiful but rather ornery creature, high-spirited with a will of her own, and she and I participate in the art of dressage, the exhibition riding in which the horse is put through a series of difficult steps and gaits, guided only by the rider's leg pressure. It is good exercise and, despite what it looks like to the uninformed eye, it is a sport that requires that the horse and rider be in perfect harmony, thinking, as it were, the same thoughts. I look past the intersection ahead and I see myself, proud on a horse's back, twenty-five years from now. I will be a bit over seventy and I imagine hearing someone say—perhaps one of my children or grandchildren—"Look how wonderfully Nancy rides. I hope I learn to ride that well someday."

∞

By the light of the moon, it is easier to talk about these things and to envision a future in which aging and feminity are linked, not separated. In the harsh sunlight, when I glance in my car mirror and realize, with just a bit of a shock, that I am no longer young, it is hard to shake off what the culture has taught me to think and feel about aging.

It will take time to change how we see ourselves and to take advantage of the path on which our sea change bodies put us, but in the circle of women, we can make progress one woman at a time. By sharing our stories, over time, the way we see ourselves as a group *will* change. Maybe then we won't find ourselves sitting in a movie theater, watching a fifty-year-old man make love to a twenty-something-year-old woman because a fifty-year-old woman isn't sexy enough.

Maybe then we will truly understand that our complicated and changing bodies have a marvelous beauty all their own that glows beneath the surface of our skins, just as the tide pool shimmers from within, by the moon's soft light.

Transitions

੭∞੭

OVER TIME, IT is not simply the path that changes but the traveler on it. The paths of the past alter our perception of the path present. Consciously, we acknowledge those major turns in the road—the moments and decisions that have literally turned the path left, right, or even backward—but there are, in addition, thousands upon thousands of small, only half-remembered moments which, taken all together over time, shape us. Transformation by experience is more like what happens to a shell or a piece of sea glass on the beach than anything else. It is the continuous flow of life's waters, wave after wave, that molds the edges of the self, not just the occasional storm.

Parts of us grow stronger, more informed, through experience. Looking back, I realize that I will never feel the crises of self-confidence that plagued me through my twenties and thirties in precisely the same way. This doesn't mean, of course, that I have a ready answer to every problem life hands me. Who does? But with a few exceptions, I can usually remember an analogous situation, and apply what I have learned from it. When I am in over my head nowadays, I know it and am able to trust my own judgment in ways I couldn't then. While conventional wisdom suggests that I have fewer choices at this stage of my life—becoming an astronaut or a ballerina or starting a new family are probably out of reach—I actually am more capable of making choices about what I do and how I do it now, and therein lies a freedom unknown to my younger self.

I have an inner compass now, a sense of direction.

The nature of the journey has shifted, too, ever so subtly. If the early part of my adult life was marked by large choices, intersections that seemed, at the time at least, to determine my course for the foreseeable future, now the path looks more like a series of transitions, the one leading to the next. It is not that the path becomes smoother or that it is without crisis; it is simply that certain of the crises seem, to adult eyes, more predictable. That the self must stay whole but flexible and ever-growing is so much more evident than it was years ago. I see the lesson confirmed in the experience of other women who, having weathered their children's childhoods and adolescence, high school and college years, find themselves out of what Anne Morrow Lindbergh called the "oyster bed": "the symbol of a spreading family and growing children" and on to another stage of life, another definition of the self.

This new stage of life may throw us off balance but, if we have hung on to our selves during those years of the balancing act that is motherhood, we will find, inevitably, a new place of centeredness. The journey teaches nothing if not the continuous reinvention of a woman's self through the stages of her life. This is precisely why it remains so important that each of us not confuse "selfishness" or "self-centeredness" with caring for the self. I have watched my mother and her friends flourish during this time of transition—rediscovering old passions and finding energy in new places—and for those of us who began our families early on in the journey, it is now our turn. My friend Diana, whose daughter is graduating from Harvard Medical School, has been able to let her own interests flourish in this time when motherhood no longer commands her attention each and every day.

For those of us who are lucky, the children we have

raised now become our friends, part of our own support system. Mary, retired from teaching, speaks of the extraordinary companionship and help her grown children have given her during the years she has cared for her aging mother, and she and her husband have passed through the various crises that aging often brings. It is a sea change worth savoring.

While my own life is still very much moored in the "oyster bed"—it is hard to imagine a house empty of children when your youngest is only six—I see the transitions express themselves in different ways. My goals have become less diffuse, more focused, and my priorities clearer. My life experience and my selfhood inform the way I practice medicine now because the knowledge I bring to a patient's bedside isn't simply drawn from my training, my medical experience, or the conferences I go to keep my skills honed. My knowledge draws on the life I've lived. Years ago, when I was trained (and too young to know any better), we were taught that the formal barriers between patient and doctor were all-important; I addressed my patients as "Mr." or "Mrs.," and they responded in kind. (Residency took this way of looking at a patient to a whole other level. "Did you check the gallbladder in 112?" we'd call out.) Life has taught me that spirit and body are one and that, for most patients, the intimacy of first names and of a question or a comment that reasserts a patient's essence and humanity in a time of trouble is part of the healing I bring. I've learned, too, to listen to my intuition, because sometimes wisdom is stored there.

Not too long ago, I had a pediatric case, a little girl of about four who needed to have her tonsils and adenoids taken out. A tonsillectomy is a routine and standard operation, one that in this day and age doesn't even require a hospital stay, and, because at-home recovery is easier on a child, I booked her on an out-patient basis. The night before the operation, I tossed and turned in bed, unusual for me particularly with an operation this routine. (I tend not to worry before an operation. Call it a surgeon's objectivity: I have plenty of experience to rely on and I trust my own skills.) But something was bothering me about the case. The girl had a history of snoring and, while we had tried a sleep study, it hadn't worked. I got to the hospital in the morning and very apologetically explained to the parents that I had decided, after all, to admit their child for an overnight stay. I told them I was sorry to complicate their lives in this way but that I felt much more comfortable proceeding with caution. I alluded to my own maternal instincts but gave them a choice: They could, if they wanted, proceed with another doctor who might well choose to operate on an out-patient basis. The parents declined, saying they trusted my judgment and wanted me on the case, so I arranged to have the child moved from one hospital, which had only out-patient facilities, to another.

The operation went without a hitch. But two hours after surgery, the little girl suddenly stopped breathing without any warning. Because she was in a hospital setting—not at home, as she well might have been—what could have been a major crisis was quickly resolved. (There's a medical reason for what happened: When the airways are obstructed, as they are with enlarged tonsils, the brain gets in the habit of sending commands to the lungs to breathe whenever the carbon dioxide levels get too high. When the obstruction is suddenly removed and there appears to be enough oxygen, the brain simply "forgets" to send the "breathe" signal.)

Was it my woman's intuition or my medical experience that informed my judgment? I honestly think it was the former, the woman's heart I have learned to trust.

I have traveled farther in some ways, since leaving Fort Wayne, than I ever imagined.

༄

But if the journey has become more predictable, it is not always easier. Throughout my life, my relationship to my parents has been a constant, and among the definitions of self I draw on for strength, certainly that of "daughter" is key among them. I speak to my parents nearly every day, sometimes just for a few minutes or so to check in and, often, for a long talk about everyday life. They are, as they always have been, a source of support, love, and sound advice (even if, historically, I haven't always listened). Because we live in different parts of the country, we make it a point to see one another four or five times a year, spending holidays and vacations together. A few years ago, an unusually long time passed between visits, and Doug, the kids, and I went "home" to Fort Wayne. That night, after everyone else went to sleep, Mom and I sat at the kitchen table together, talking about everything and nothing, having tea. It is a familiar ritual since my teenage years, when we lived in the old house on North Washington Road, and Mom and I would talk late into the night. It was the first circle of women I ever belonged to. This particular night, I suddenly saw that my mother was older than I ever realized. The image I had in my heart was the way she had looked during my early adulthood and, perhaps because we had been apart and because talking on the telephone and hearing an unchanged and familiar voice lets us see with our imagination, I never had had to adjust it. (My inner image of myself probably dates from the same period, some twenty years ago.) In that instant of clarity, when I actually saw the deeper lines on her face, the visible and more subtle changes time had wrought, I realized how completely unprepared I was and probably always will be to give her or my father up.

For all that I understand the rhythm of life, the cycle of birth, aging, and death, facing it is another matter entirely. Of all the passages the necessary journey includes, this is among the most difficult. It is a passage that, for some of us, will bring the gift of spiritual growth, but always at great cost. I suppose the loss of our parents is the final stage of growing up, the logical extension of that first moment when we begin to break away from our childhood selves and set out into the world alone, but that doesn't help me when I think about it. It is simply too painful, even now, to contemplate.

Yet I have learned from other women that even this hard moment in life has things to teach us about resolution, endings, selfhood, and, most important, about love. My friend Cindy—equestrienne, lawyer and agent, deal-maker supreme—lost her mother to a congenital heart defect when she was seventeen and still in high school. Her mother's illness set the rhythm of her childhood and, by the time she was a pre-teenager, Cindy had become her mother's caretaker, talking to her doctors, managing her medications, and making decisions about her welfare. (These duties fell to her, as they often do to girls and women, because she was female and because there was no one else to do it. Her brother had married and moved away and her father had been left reeling by his wife's illness and the awful possibility that she might die. Their relationship was a deep and loving one, and the thought of losing her left him emotionally paralyzed and afraid to act.) When it became clear that her mother needed surgery to survive, Cindy called the Mayo Clinic and arranged for her mother to be taken by ambulance from Chicago, where they lived, to Rochester, Minnesota.

Her mother died there, still only in her early fifties, and Cindy never got the chance to say good-bye.

Cindy's sense of loss was enormous. Without a final leave-taking, Cindy was deprived of closure; the process of mourning and grieving, which is part of healing, was cut off. Her relationship with her mother stayed frozen in time, that of a parent and a child not yet full-grown, and as a result, despite Cindy's many successes, she felt rudderless during her twenties, thirties, and forties, still searching for the mother she had lost. Five years ago, when her father died, Cindy found herself parentless and, despite all the years of being alone in all the ways that mattered, she grieved deeply. For the first time, she grieved for her mother as well as her father. And grieving set her free.

At this point in her life, there isn't a day that Cindy doesn't find herself talking to her mother. When we have deals that go well, Cindy is always quick to say that her mother must be watching over both of us. She has come to know that her mother is proud of her, of her achievements, of her success, and of the woman she has become. And for all of that, she feels her mother's loss more meaningfully than ever.

Sometimes, the lesson of this transition reaches beyond the individual and speaks to another kind of truth. Jane, a sculptor, publishing executive, and the mother of a daughter now in her twenties, found her own life intertwined with her mother's in ways she had never anticipated. As she points out, we often find ourselves unprepared for all the consequences of the extended lifetime that medical advances have given our elders. Jane's long-widowed mother, a pretty and vivacious woman, had remained active, vital, and autonomous until her eightieth year when, suddenly, she began to exhibit symptoms of dementia. A battery of tests revealed not Alzheimer's, as Jane had originally feared, but a progressive disease, caused by hardening of the arteries. As it turned out, her mother's journey out of this world and into another took years to complete and, because it did, the journey was one shared by two generations of women, albeit in different ways.

Since Jane's adolescence, their relationship had been marked by ambivalence, and Jane's initial entry into this new role of caretaker brought many of those feelings out into the open. But over time, what began as enforced intimacy yielded to something truer. Jane came to enjoy her and her company. And, as her mother aged and the disease broke down the barriers between her conscious and unconscious lives, Jane gained greater insight into the woman who had given her life. By the end, their relationship had been resolved and Jane was able, without ambivalence, to love, honor, and mourn her. In the small rhythms of the tasks she performed for her mother—balancing her checkbooks, paying bills, going grocery shopping for her—and in the activities they shared—eating together, reading children's books, and making art together—Jane discovered not the sense of duty and obligation that had originally motivated her but something more important.

Birth and death are both doorways, in and out of human experience, and as Jane puts it, each is "sacral in nature." Traditionally, the management of birth and death has been the territory of women, and Jane now sees her involvement in her mother's death not as obligation but as an honor. She feels her experience connected her to the patterns of the cosmos, where she was able to help her mother go to the place of transition, the doorway out, in company. It was a difficult experience, she admits, including the weeks she spent sorting through the things in her mother's apartment. She remembers the loss she felt, handling the objects her mother had lived with, even catching the scent of her mother's perfume on a blouse or handkerchief. But by doing the work of caretaking, Jane closed the circle, linking beginnings and endings, birth and death, as they are in the greater scheme.

She looks back at this period of her life with only a single regret: that, in the end, she allowed her mother to be sent to a hospital. It was, she says, a mistake and, had she had it to do over, she would know now that the extension of life medical intervention offered her mother—a few extra weeks—was not what her mother needed.

In the journey shared, there was closure. The portrait of her mother—young, vibrant, with the world before her—hangs where it belongs: in Jane's bedroom.

∞

The link between beginnings and endings is the hardest lesson the journey has to teach us. On a literal and practical level, the combination of medical advances that prolong human life (over the course of the last century, life expectancy went from forty-five years to seventy-nine) and the postponement of childbearing sometimes make the generations overlap in ways that are uncomfortable and hard to deal with. Women in their late forties and early fifties, with young children still at home, find themselves dealing with aging parents who can no longer be independent. Mary, whose daughter bore her first child at the age of almost forty, finds herself torn between her grandchildren and her ninety-eight-year-old mother. She is, as she puts it, "squashed" between conflicting demands, at a time in her life when her own energy has very real limits. All of this is complicated by the fact that our society as a whole, as Mary Pipher points out in her book *Another Country*, is culturally hostile toward the old and remains without the facilities or resources to help make aging part of everyday life.

But there is more to the problem our culture has with beginnings and endings than even that. Perhaps it is the way we measure and understand the life journey that makes it so hard for us to learn what we need to in the times of transition. We tend to see the journey and our growth as linear. We begin, as children, understanding growth in a literal way, when our parents mark our height with chalk or pencil on the wall. In time, we measure our children, our paychecks, our progress, and our achievements with the same metaphorical chalk marks. But the journey isn't linear. We need instead to learn from both the cycles of our female bodies and all the small endings that accompany our growth—the aging of the eggs we're born with, the slow depletion of neurons, the loss of height we will all experience—that beginnings and endings are inseparable.

And perhaps then, and only then, we will fully be able to learn from those necessary parts of the journey, including the ones where pain and letting go become part of the knowledge we bring to our tomorrows.

In the Circle of Women

∽

EVERY EXPERIENCE CHANGES us in small ways and large. I've grown by writing this book, and what I learned from writing it has become a part of the necessary journey the book describes. I hope that reading it has helped you think about your own journey, those necessary passages and intersections, and that you will follow my example by telling your stories as I have told mine.

Thousands of years ago, as women did the work of sustaining their families and children, whether gathering food or weaving clothes and baskets or nursing their young, they told stories both to entertain themselves and to give themselves a context. They created tales of how the world around them was created, and how the life they lived came to be. Weaving a narrative, then and now, gives meaning and resonance to the details of daily existence.

I think stories play a particular role in the lives of women, who are storytellers by nature. We invent ourselves through the process of storytelling. Our children beg us for stories about their beginnings to help define themselves, while the stories of our own childhoods, in turn, help our children begin to understand how we became the women we are. The stories our parents and grandparents told us shaped us as girls, taught us lessons about family and behavior, and endowed us, along the way, with a unique personal history. We read books and magazines, watch television, go to plays and movies in search of stories that are not about us but help us grapple with the important issues of life as well as entertain us. Stories support, heal, and, above all, inspire us.

If we can teach ourselves to be listeners, we will discover that, in the circle of women, there is a wealth of knowledge, insight, and help available to us. In the stories and the lives of all women—not just the famous or accomplished—there are lessons of value that can help us all dream a better future.

On my desk, alongside pictures of my two daughters, there is a framed, grainy black-and-white photograph. In it, a smiling young woman sits in a small wooden wagon, wearing a long, figured-print dress that was the basic wardrobe in the Midwest in the early twentieth century. Her eyes squint in the bright sunlight. The sleeves of her dress are pushed up above her elbows, and she seems comfortable and relaxed. Behind her is another woman, wearing an apron over her dress, her arms folded tight against her body. Her face turned toward the camera, she is stern and unsmiling. On the side of the wagon, painted in rough white letters, are the words "Votes for Women, Omaha, Ne., 1915."

The girl in the wagon was my grandmother, and the woman behind her was her mother, the great-grandmother I never knew. There are many other stories my grandmother told first my mother and then me but, oddly, the story of their involvement in getting women the vote wasn't one of them. The photograph was found in a dusty old box, over seventy years after it was taken, after my grandmother died.

The picture reminds me that I come from a line of strong, resilient women, which continues on with my own daughters. But, upon reflection, I see that there is another story this photograph tells.

The lives of my foremothers were harder than the one I've lived. My great-grandmother, a German immigrant, had little or no formal education. She finally taught herself to read rudimentary English but never to write it. My grandmother finished eighth grade and soon married a journeyman laborer who, during the Depression, moved wherever the jobs were, his wife and four children in tow. On a daily basis, each of these two women worried about where the next meal would come from and how their children would be clothed. They laundered, cleaned, tended, and managed, without mechanical or any other kind of help, save that of family. They bartered to get their children extras. Their entertainments were dictated by expenses: a hand of cards, perhaps, or a story read out loud. Their home-sewn dresses were fashioned from yard goods bought at porch sales or altered from used clothing.

But despite all that occupied these women in the day-to-day—the seemingly endless chores and concerns—the photograph tells me that they also managed to perceive themselves as playing a part in a better future. The words on the little wagon—"Votes for Women"—testify to the fact that both of them understood themselves as belonging to a community of women, made up of neighbors and strangers alike, who needed a voice in their own destinies. Where they were in life didn't stop them from being able to imagine where they—and the generations of women that would follow—could be.

While it's easy to forget now, five generations of

voting women later, the battle for and against giving women the vote had been pitched in Nebraska, as it was in many other states. Identifying themselves with the suffragist cause was, in 1915, a gutsy move for these two women who lived on the margins of Nebraska society. Just a year before the photograph was taken, in 1914, a state amendment that would have granted the vote had been roundly defeated. Opponents of voting rights included not just men but women who favored the status quo. Many, though not all, of the "Antis," as they called themselves, were well-to-do women from established, well-known families, and there is inspiration in the example of my foremothers, in their home-sewn dresses, believing in themselves and in women enough to take a stand against them.

In 1917 Nebraska voted to give women partial suffrage, allowing them to vote for president. In 1920 the Nineteenth Amendment was passed. My grandmother lived to see her daughter go to college and her granddaughter graduate from medical school and become a doctor. Her great-granddaughters, my children, will have opportunities undreamed of one hundred years ago.

But the work of imagining a different, better future for all women isn't done. If we are to change how women think and feel about themselves in the new century and the new millennium, we need to work together. There is still much to do.

As women, we need to see ourselves as belonging to a community that needs the help and talent of every individual within it to thrive and prosper. We must take it upon ourselves to mentor the youngest members of our community and teach them the lessons of the journeys we have taken. We need to help young women discover the potential within themselves by going into the grade schools, middle schools, and high schools and telling our girls that they can be anything they want to be.

If we can begin to think as a community of women, we will, in time, understand that they are *our* girls, and that the responsibility for helping them realize their dreams is *ours*.

As mothers, sisters, aunts, and grandmothers, we need to teach our sons, brothers, nephews, and grandsons to respect and honor women's special gifts. If we are to change the cultural stereotypes that continue to hobble our girls, then we must also address the way stereotypes hurt our boys. One of the challenges ahead in my own personal journey is that of raising my son to be a caring, sensitive individual who will be secure enough in his own gifts and abilities not to be threatened by those of a woman.

We need to address the social issues that adversely affect women and children in their daily lives and that make the journey for those less privileged more perilous than it needs to be. We must, as a community, insist that affordable health insurance and care be made available for everyone in America.

We need, as workers and citizens, to lobby for equal pay for equal work. We must find our political voices and exercise our votes.

Like my foremothers, I believe fervently in the community of women. I believe that more connects us to each other than separates us, regardless of the choices we have made in our lives. For the last ten years or so, I've lectured all around the country and have met hundreds and hundreds of women, all of whom are different from one another but with whom I have always felt a connection. I think our collective experience as women links us.

Perhaps when we come to recognize the common bond that exists among all women, we will all be able to take pride in ourselves and in each other. Perhaps then, in the new millennium, we can raise a glass to both the things that make us different and the things that make us, under the skin, sisters at heart.

Acknowledgments

∾

Sometimes, gifts fall from the sky; and others, they are harder won. This book brought me a multitude of gifts. By writing about and giving voice to my own passages, I was able to see my own mistakes in another light. I was able to forgive anew. And I learned something more about hope. I was also, on these pages, to say thank you in a different, more articulate way.

First and foremost, everything is due to my parents. I need not say more. And to Martha, my sister, who knows what she has given me, I hope I have given it back in kind. To the larger circle of friends, some men, but mostly women: Thanks again, particularly for those times when the truth was hard to face, and when I wasn't likable. In no particular order, Diana, Connie, Cindy: I do not know where I would be without you. To Brenda and Sam, who picked up every piece I dropped when Kate was a baby: I am so proud that you are her godparents.

To all the fellows of group VIII of the Kellogg National Fellowship Program: I can't imagine this life without you. We have traveled the world, shared each other's secrets, and have been the truest support system imaginable. Being a Kellogg fellow was—is—a cornerstone of my survival. To the golfies who gave me the first glimpse of true camaraderie; to those who helped push my pregnant body on and off buses in Brazil; to the women who helped me give Rachel her middle name above the fjords in Bergen; to Chris, who believed in me all the way: I love you.

On the homefront: love and thanks to all who let me put myself and my work on the front burner. I know—and you know—who you are: Casandra, Angie, Debby, and Molly. And, finally, an answer to all those who ask how I can continue to practice medicine while taking on the rest, a simple answer: my partner, Dr. Dan Hartman. His skills and support make it possible. Not a day goes by without my thanking every star for his surgical skills and friendship.

And now, to the book itself. Meeting and working with Peg Streep was an unforeseen part of the work but it turned out to be a true collaboration in every sense of the word. We found ourselves during countless hours of phone calls, during dinners and on street corners, and ended up finishing each other's sentences. Once again, the circle of women mattered: We each found, in each other's lives, things of meaning and value, and things each of us was blind to. Her insight, intellect, and passion have made finishing this book bittersweet, but I am lucky to walk away with her friendship. She is a broad in the truest sense of the word.

Thank you to Mary Ellen O'Neill, my editor, and to Martha Levin at Hyperion, who were able to see beyond the science of women's mental health and give me free rein. I know the book surprised them, but, they were steadfast in their guidance and support. Thanks too to Bob Miller and the rest of the folks at Hyperion for their expertise and support.

Thank you to Leslie Garisto for the editorial blue pencil, to Liza Dawson for introducing to me to Peg, and to Peg's friends, Erika Rosenfeld, Jane Lahr, and Mary Eve Finestone, for their advice and stories.

Resources

This is an informal rather than comprehensive listing of books and organizations that may be useful to women at different stages of their journeys, keyed into the chapters of this book.

Please note, however, that these resources are meant to provide a guide to information only; in no case should you embark on a course of treatment or action without consulting your health-care professional.

Books of Interest

Brown, Lyn Mikel and Carol Gilligan. *Meeting at the Crossroads: Women's Psychology and Girls' Development.* New York: Ballantine Books, 1992.

Edelman, Hope. *Motherless Daughters: The Legacy of Loss.* New York: Dell Publishing, 1994.

Edelman, Marian Wright. *Lanterns: A Memoir of Mentors.* Boston: Beacon Press, 1999.

Gilligan, Carol. *In a Different Voice: Psychological Theory and Women's Development.* Cambridge, MA: Harvard University Press, 1982.

Greer, Germaine. *The Change: Women, Aging, and the Menopause.* New York: Alfred A. Knopf, 1992.

Lindbergh, Anne Morrow. *Gift from the Sea.* New York: Pantheon Books, 1997.

Orenstein, Peggy (in association with the American Association of University Women). *Schoolgirls: Young Women, Self-Esteem, and the Confidence Gap.* New York: Anchor Books, 1994.

Peck, M. Scott, M.D. *The Road Less Traveled: A New Psychology of Love, Traditional Values, and Spiritual Growth.* New York: Touchstone, 1978.

Pipher, Mary, Ph.D. *Another Country: Navigating the Emotional Terrain of Our Elders.* New York: Riverhead, 1999.

———*Reviving Ophelia: Saving the Lives of Adolescent Girls.* New York: G. P. Putnam's Sons, 1994.

Reps, Paul. *Zen Flesh, Zen Bones: A Collection of Zen and Pre-Zen Writings.* Garden City, NY: Doubleday & Co., 1961.

Rich, Adrienne. *Of Woman Born: Motherhood as an Experience and Institution.* New York: W. W. Norton & Company, 1986.

Rubenstein, Carin, Ph.D. *The Sacrificial Mother: Escaping the Trap of Self-Denial.* New York: Hyperion, 1998.

Sheehy, Gail. *The Silent Passage: Menopause.* New York: Random House, 1992.

Siegel, Bernie S., M.D. *Love, Medicine, & Miracles: Lessons Learned about Self-Healing from a Surgeon's Experience with Exceptional Patients.* New York: HarperPerennial, 1998.

Snyderman, Nancy L., M.D. *Dr. Nancy Snyderman's Guide to Good Health: What Every Forty-Plus Woman Should Know about Her Changing Body.* New York: William Morrow and Company, Inc., 1996.

Thurer, Shari L. *The Myths of Motherhood: How Culture Reinvents the Good Mother.* Boston and New York:

Houghton Mifflin Company, 1994.

Warner, Marina. *From the Beast to the Blonde: On Fairy Tales and Their Tellers*. New York: Farrar, Straus & Giroux, 1994.

Blind Alleys

The RAINN (Rape, Abuse & Incest National Network) has a 24-hour hotline to reach the nearest crisis center (1-800-656-HOPE) *for immediate help*, or you can search for a crisis center on the Internet at www.rainn.org.

Check the pages of your local telephone book as well.

Inspirations

The Ms. Foundation, in addition to sponsoring and creating "Take Our Daughters to Work Day," funds "girl-driven" programs all over the country. Write the Ms. Foundation at 120 Wall Street, New York, NY 10005 (212-742-2300), or visit the website at www.ms.foundation.org (you can e-mail them, too, at info@ms.foundation.org).

Girls Incorporated is a fifty-year-old national youth organization with programs for girls. For information either visit their website (www.girlsinc.org) or write or call Girls Incorporated National Headquarters, 120 Wall Street, 3rd floor, New York, NY 10005 (212-509-2000), or Girls Incorporated National Resource Center, 441 West Michigan Street, Indianapolis, IN 46202-3233 (317-634-7546).

Mirror Images

Information on issues pertaining to girls' self-esteem and eating disorders is available from a wide variety of sources. The

American Association of University Women, 1111 Sixteenth Street, N.W., Washington, D.C. 20036 (800-326-AAUW), has ongoing studies pertaining to self-esteem; they can also be reached on-line at www.aauw.org.

For eating disorders, contact the National Association of Anorexia Nervosa and Associated Disorders on the Internet at www.anad.org or call or write them at ANAD, P.O. Box 7, Highland Park, IL 60035 (847-831-3438).

For information on psychological problems associated with girls and adolesence, contact the American Psychological Association, 750 First Street, N.E., Washington, D.C. 20002-4242 (202-336-5500) or on the Internet at www.apa.org.

The American Academy of Child and Adolescent Psychiatry is also a good source of information; write or call at 3615 Wisconsin Avenue, N.W., Washington, D.C. 20016 (202-966-7300), or on the Internet, www.aacap.org.

A Change of Direction

For all manner of help and information (as well as inspiration and counseling) on starting and maintaining a business—from mentoring by successful women entrepreneurs to state-of-the art technology and business software—contact the Office of Women's Business Ownership, 409 Third Street, S.W., 4th floor, Washington, D.C. 20416 (202-205-6673) or the Small Business Administration at 1-800-8-ASK-SBA. On the Internet, find them at www.sba.gov/womeninbusiness.

Wake-up Calls

The American Cancer Society (1-800-ACS-2345, toll-free and 24 hours a day) is a source of all types of information about all types of cancer. On the Internet, find them at www.cancer.org for general information as well as local resources for your area.

The National Institute of Health, a government agency, is a reliable source of information pertaining to many diseases. It has its own website pertaining to cancer at cancernet. nci.nih.gov. For more, see the information on MEDLINE plus, below, under "Moon Magic."

The Cancer Research Institute (681 Fifth Avenue, New York, NY 10022) can be reached by toll-free telephone (1-800-99CANCER or 1-800-992-2623) or on the Internet at www.cancerresearch.org.

For information on heart disease, contact the national center of the American Heart Association, 7272 Greenville Avenue, Dallas, TX 75231. For heart and stroke information, call 1-800-AHA-USA1. For women's health information, call 1-888-MY-HEART. On the Internet, www.americanheart.org.

The National Women's Health Information Center offers information (over 3,000 free publications) on over 800 different medical problems, as well as referrals to other sources of information. You can write them at The National Women's Health Information Center, 8550 Arlington Blvd., Suite 300, Fairfax, VA 22031 or call at 703-560-6619. You can contact an information specialist, Monday through Friday, 9 a.m. to 6 p.m. EST (excluding federal holidays) at 1-800-994-WOMAN. On the Internet, contact them at www.4woman.gov.

Into the Labyrinth

The National Institute of Mental Health, part of the government's NIH, has free brochures and pamphlets on both general and specific mental health issues, as well as guides to the latest in mental health research. For on-line information, find it at www.nimh.nih.gov. For information, call 301-443-4513 or write The National Institute of Mental Health, 60001 Executive Boulevard, Room 8181, MSC9663, Betheseda, MD 20892. For free brochures on depression and its treatment (as well as other brochures) call 800-421-4211.

The American Psychiatric Association also has pamphlets and brochures available to the public; write or call them at The American Psychiatric Association, 1400 K Street, N.W., Washington, D.C. 20005 (202-682-6000). Their series of pamphlets, "Let's Talk about the Facts," is designed to reduce the stigmas surrounding mental illnesses. On the Internet, their address is www.psych.org.

Another source is the National Mental Health Association, 1021 Prince Street, Alexandria, VA 22314-2971 (800-969-NMHA). On the Internet, www. nmha.org.

Moon Magic

For information on menopause and other women's health issues, try the NIH's Medline plus health information (on-line at www.nlm.nih.gov/medlineplus) or by mail contact the U.S. National Library of Medicine, 8600 Rockville Pike, Betheseda, MD 20892.

Planned Parenthood also has information on menopause and other aspects of women's health. Contact them at one of the following addresses: Planned Parenthood Federation of America, 810 Seventh Avenue, New York, NY 10019 (212-541-7800); Planned Parenthood Federation of America, 1 Oakbrook Terrace, #808, Oakbrook Terrace, IL 60181 (630-627-9549); Planned Parenthood Federation of America, 333 Broadway, San Francisco, CA 94133 (415-956-3331);

Planned Parenthood of America, 2230 Connecticut Avenue N.W., #461, Washington, D.C. 20036 (202-293-4349). On the Internet, find them at www.plannedparenthood.org. For medical advice or to schedule an appointment with the Planned Parenthood office near you, call 800-230-PLAN.

The American College of Obstetricians and Gynecologists (ACOG) is also a source of information about menopause and related matters; write them at 409 12 Street S.W., P.O. Box 96920, Washington, D.C. 20090-6920 or find them on the Internet at www.acog.org.

The North American Menopause Society is a nonprofit organization dedicated to promoting the understanding of menopause, and supplying unbiased and accurate information to health providers and the public. Write The North American Menopause Society, P.O. Box 94527, Cleveland, OH 44101-4527, call 440-442-7550, or find them on the Internet at www. menopause.org.

See also The National Women's Health Information Center under "Wake-Up Calls" above.

Transitions

The National Institute on Aging, part of the NIH, is the clearinghouse for information pertaining to health and aging, and can be reached on-line at www.nih.gov-nia. For information on Alzheimer's, you can contact the Alzheimer's Disease Education and Referral Center (ADEAR) by mail at P.O. Box 8250, Silver Spring, MD 20907-8250, by telephone at 800-438-4380, or by e-mail at adear@alzheimers.org. The website is www.alzheimers.org.

For information on services available to the elderly, contact the

Administration on Aging, 3330 Independence Avenue S.W., Washington, D.C. 20201. By telephone, contact the Eldercare Locator to find local services for an older person at 800-766-1116. For technical information, call the AOA's National Aging Information Center at 202-619-7501.

On the Internet, you can find Access America for Seniors (www.seniors.gov), a site that has all the government services grouped together.